Soups
& Salads
for Spring and Summer Days

KID-PLEASING RECIPES

Soups & Salads
for Spring and Summer Days

KID-PLEASING RECIPES

LIZA FOSBURGH

BERKSHIRE HOUSE PUBLISHERS
Lee, Massachusetts

SOUPS & SALADS FOR SPRING AND SUMMER DAYS:
Kid-Pleasing Recipes
Copyright © 2002 by Berkshire House Publishers
All rights reserved.

Library of Congress Cataloging-in-Publication Data

Fosburgh, Liza.
Soups & salads for spring and summer days: kid-pleasing recipes / Liza Fosburgh.
        p. cm.
Includes index.
ISBN 1-58157-059-7
1. Soups. 2. Salads. I. Title.

TX757.F66 2002
641.8'13'—dc21

                                                                        2001043742

ISBN: 1-58157-059-7

Editor: Dale Evva Gelfand
Cover and book design: Jane McWhorter, Blue Sky Productions.

On the front cover: photography by A. Blake Gardner. Counterclockwise from top: Abbie's Chicken Salad with Grapes; Spinach, Corn, and Red Onion Salad; Basil-Tomato Medley; Asparagus and Lemon Soup with Orzo.

Berkshire House books are available at substantial discounts for bulk purchases by corporations and other organizations for promotions and premiums. Special personalized editions can also be produced in large quantities. For more information, contact:

Berkshire House Publishers
480 Pleasant St., Suite 5, Lee, MA 01238
800-321-8526
E-mail: info@berkshirehouse.com
Website: www.berkshirehouse.com

Printed in the United States of America
10 9 8 7 6 5 4 3 2 1

Contents

Cook's Preface

Where I live, in a hollow carved between the Taconic Mountains and the Berkshire Mountains in upstate New York, the growing season is very short. Traditionally, it is unwise to plant tender annuals outside before Memorial Day — the foolhardy who have tried to defy these age-old words of wisdom have rued the day that they thought they knew better — and there is apt to be a frost any time after Labor Day. Stalwart perennials have learned over the generations to dig their roots deep into the ground and bow their heads before the chill winds and frosty dews, but those delicate-leaved annuals like basil, peppers, and tomatoes need June, July, and August weather to help them grow and be bountiful.

Where I grew up in the South, it was an entirely different matter. The growing season was for most of the year. As a result of the warm soil and warmer air, we had fresh vegetables every day and learned to love them at a very early age. It's possible that my family had more vegetables than most. My father was a doctor in an area that was mostly farmland, and in those times when the major income-producing crops were poor — either ruined by rain or stunted by drought — he would be paid for his medical services with home-grown and homemade things. Occasionally it was a hand-tatted lace tablecloth or a splendid handmade broom, but usually payment came in the form of vegetables from the farmer's kitchen garden. My mother, a gracious Southern lady, always received these sacks and baskets of vegetables with a smile and warm words of thanks, as if they were the very things she wanted most in the world. As a result, we had a lot of vegetable dishes at dinner as well as vegetable soups and salads. My brother and I learned to enjoy vegetables, and that pleasure has lasted us all of our lives.

My mother loved to make soups. She almost relished hearing of someone who had taken to a sickbed so she could whip up a nourishing batch of vegetable soup. Since she had inside information of this nature, she was in the kitchen a lot, pushing aside the cook and combining rich stocks, fresh vegetables, thick cream, and anything else she deemed necessary for a full recovery. The soup would be put up in big jars, wrapped in thick towels, and tucked in a basket. One of us children would get the job of riding in the backseat of her big LaSalle to steady the basket as we sped through town or out across the countryside. She never stayed inside the sick house very long (we always had to wait in the car) and soon emerged with the basket and towel, ready for the next patient to fall, convinced that her nutritional ministrations were almost as valuable as our father's pills and poultices.

Salads were frequently served at our house and always on picnics. There is so much more variety now — any limits are in the cook's imagination — but those old-fashioned salads we used to have are still as good as ever, using fresh lettuces, beans, cabbages, cucumbers, potatoes, and sweet onions. I'm not sure what oils and vinegars were used back then, but I do remember that the mayonnaise was homemade — and not in the blender or food processor as I now make it but by hand with a silver fork (and probably using bartered eggs that had just been delivered that morning.)

A book on soups and salads could also be called The Joy of Vegetables.

Here in the North, my two sons learned at an early age to help in my vegetable garden. They usually got their best friend to help with this annual event, and the three of them seemed to enjoy sowing, making sure the rows were straight and properly spaced and the seeds exactly dribbled into the depressions. They willingly helped later on, too, sliding along between the rows to weed or among the mature produce to pick. Now grown up with families of their own, they continue to cultivate vegetables, one in a city garden and the other in a sunny area of his lawn in a town outside a city.

I have now gone from a very large vegetable garden to a more modest one because a lot of my spare time has now gone into the care of flowers. But between my own vegetables and those at local markets, I have plenty all spring and summer, and my interest in cooking — especially soups and salads — has not waned.

I hope all cooks enjoy their time in the kitchen as much as I do. As always, I encourage you to be creative and try new things. I do, and it's always a pleasure and usually a treat.

Part I
SOUPS

Most kids like soup if it is appealing-looking and delicious. My children always liked soup, especially a chunky one, and now my grandchildren are following suit. There are a few basic rules I stick by, and they seem to work in most cases. For example, it's all right to mince parsley and use it as a garnish for adults, but little ones don't like unidentifiable green things floating on top of their food. If parsley is to be used, leave it as a whole sprig and place it on the soup like a flower decoration — kids will simple eat around it. Color is also important: browns, grays, and tans are best avoided; reds, yellows, and bright greens are cheerful and acceptable. Croutons and little oyster crackers are fun and liked by all; crushed red pepper and tiny bits of jalapeño peppers are for adults only.

These things are borne of common sense, as is the tastiness of the soup pot. As always, I recommend being adventurous and experimenting — but with a level head and the tastes of kids and adults foremost in mind — especially those of the kids.

Happy cooking!

Specialty Soups

In the cooking world, these soups would probably fall into the medley department, though "roundup" might be a better description. Some of them should be served hot; others, cold. Remember that even on the steamiest summer day, a hot hamburger or a roasted vegetable — whether from the grill or the stove — is quite tasty, and the same goes for soups. The English in India drank hot tea every afternoon and, copying their native hosts, ate hot and spicy curries as one of their staples. So why not anyone anywhere?

I have found that many grown-ups prefer hot to cold for all foods, and maybe the reason is that hot foods, psychologically speaking, are more filling. On the other hand, kids, who have a lot of distractions, questions, and comments about almost anything in their inquisitive minds (especially at the table), are apt to fool around with hot food on the plate for so long that it turns cold before it reaches their mouths. So temperature is no problem for them either way.

On a midsummer day, if it's too steamy in the kitchen to keep something hot on the stove, go ahead and let it cool to warm or room temperature. Butter in the pot will still be liquid, and milk won't have taken on a life of its own. Remember, the comfort of the cook is a major factor when preparing food.

Cheese and Chili Peppers

This is one of those times when you have to use your own judgment about the adventurous tastes of your eaters. Some adults like very hot and spicy foods, while others prefer milder fare. Certainly the same goes for kids. In this recipe, if you want a really hot taste, the kind that brings tears to your eyes, mince some extra peppers and serve them separately on a little plate. It's usually better to be safe than sorry.

Last summer I discovered the wonderful Hungarian wax peppers, which have a little bite but don't burn your tongue. They are easy to grow, either in a vegetable garden or in a big pot on a terrace. I ate them with abandon, slicing them into sandwiches and salads alike as well as putting a thin slice on a cracker spread with cream cheese. Many good produce markets now carry them, and they are a treat if you can find them. So if you want a blander hot pepper taste, use a Hungarian wax pepper instead of the jalapeño listed below.

1 hot green pepper, such as jalapeño, minced.
3 tablespoons butter or margarine
3 egg yolks, beaten until frothy
3 cups chicken stock, heated to boiling
4 tablespoons grated cheddar cheese

Sauté the pepper in the butter until just limp and set aside. Add about ¼ cup of the hot stock to the egg yolks, stirring vigorously, and blend well. Add another ¼ cup of stock and blend well again. Then gradually stir the beaten egg yolks into the remaining hot stock in a saucepan, stirring constantly over a low heat until soup is slightly thickened. Do not overcook — scrambled eggs are not the desired end result here. Stir in the cheese, blending well, until it is melted. Remove from heat. Add the sautéed pepper, season to taste with salt, and serve immediately while it is hot.

Makes about 6 half-cup servings.

If you're using this soup as a first course, follow it with something mild and soothing, such as a wholesome salad like Ziti with Mushrooms, Ginger, and Tuna, and top it off with a wonderful summer sherbet for dessert. All ages will like this meal.

Cold Egg Cream

If you want to get out of the kitchen on a hot day, make this soup ahead of time and refrigerate. It's good with a hearty vegetable side dish such as Spinach, Corn, and Red Onion Salad, some dense grain bread, and fresh fruit. The little ones as well as the adults in my family like this as a good summer meal. We like to sit around the picnic table with the food arranged down the middle of the table as we talk and listen to the sounds of summer while we eat.

I never much cared for buttermilk as a drink when I was a child — and still don't. My mother frequently drank it on a hot summer day, praising its chilly pleasures, but she failed to convince me. However, I do like its subtle tangy taste when it's hidden in the midst of other ingredients like cold soups. If members of your family don't like it, either don't tell them these ingredients, or fib a bit and say it's whole milk and sour cream — which isn't too far from the true facts, anyway.

4 hard-boiled eggs, grated or minced
¼ cup mayonnaise
1 cup buttermilk
1 sweet onion such as Vidalia, minced
1 celery stalk, minced
¼ cup minced parsley
¼ cup minced chives
1 teaspoon curry powder

Combine all the ingredients in a bowl, season to taste with salt and pepper, and chill. Serve cold.

Makes 6 to 8 small servings.

Okroshka

An unusual and superb soup of Russian origin, this recipe was given to me by Josephine Terry Brune, who got it from the late Harold Hochschild. The end result should be cream colored and the liquid creamy. In Russia, a special type of cider is used; here, ginger ale. Adventurous kids who like crunchy raw vegetables will like it, too. I like it with hot cornbread on the side, but a dense grain bread or black bread also work well.

2 hard-cooked eggs, whites chopped and yolks mashed
1 cup diced ham
1 cup diced cooked chicken or turkey
½ cup finely chopped radishes
½ cup finely chopped scallions
1 small cucumber, peeled, large seeds removed, and chopped
1 tablespoon minced fresh dillweed
¼ teaspoon dry mustard
¼ cup buttermilk (a mix of whole milk and plain yogurt may be substituted)
¾ cup sour cream
1 ½ 7-ounce bottles ice-cold ginger ale

Combine the chopped egg whites, ham, chicken or turkey, radishes, scallions, cucumber, and dill in a bowl. Chill. In a separate bowl, make a soupy puree of the egg yolks, mustard, and buttermilk. Blend in the sour cream. Chill. When ready to serve, combine both mixtures and stir in the ginger ale. Season to taste. Serve very cold.

Makes 9 or 10 cups

Peppery Summer Beef

This recipe is adapted from an old recipe of mine using an oxtail. I used to have a cattle-raising neighbor who very kindly gave me a tail when a steer was sent to its final resting place. Now those tails are too hard to find and, to me, not worth the search. (Cooks on Midwestern farms and city dwellers have more access to these; suburbanites and ordinary country folk are at a disadvantage.) So I use stewing beef instead. Besides, kids are more apt to eat this soup if it's made with beef chunks.

1 pound stewing beef chunks
3 tablespoons flour mixed with a little salt and pepper
1 tablespoon bacon fat (or butter or margarine)
2 quarts beef stock (or canned beef broth), heated
mixture of minced fresh herbs (1 bay leaf, 2 sprigs each of thyme, marjoram, and parsley)
6 or 7 whole cloves, tied in a cloth bag, or 1 teaspoon ground cloves
1 tablespoon coarsely ground black pepper
½ cup chopped scallions (green tops as well as the white bulb)
2 medium-size carrots, sliced
1 ½ cups sliced green beans
1 ½ cup chopped celery
1 ½ cups green peas, fresh or frozen
4 or 5 large ripe tomatoes, peeled and chopped
1 garlic clove, minced
1 cup small-size macaroni (uncooked)

In a bowl, toss the beef chunks with the flour mixture to coat. Melt the bacon fat or butter in a large heavy pot and brown the coated beef. Stir in any remaining flour. Gradually add the beef stock, stirring, and cook gently to slightly thicken. Add the herbs, cloves, and black pepper and simmer gently, covered, for 2 ½ hours. Add the vegetables and garlic and cook for another ½ hour. Discard the cloves bag. Add the macaroni and cook for another 15 to 20 minutes or until tender. Season to taste with salt and pepper. Serve hot.

Makes 3 ½ to 4 quarts

For all ages. Serve with a simple green salad such as Greens with Apples and Feta.

Senegalese, More or Less

The egg yolks, curry powder, milk, and chicken stock are pretty basic for this soup. The addition of apple juice, chicken bits, carrots, and potatoes adds a little extra. My grandchildren eat this without hesitation. It's good with a fruit salad such as Pears, Apples, and Pecans on Endive Spears.

2 egg yolks
½ teaspoon curry powder (or more to taste)
1 cup whole milk
2 cups chicken stock, heated
½ cup minced peeled, cooked potatoes (this is the time to use a
  leftover cooked potato)
½ cup grated carrots
½ cup apple juice
½ cup finely minced cooked chicken
¼ cup sherry (for adults; additional apple juice for the young)

Beat together the egg yolks, curry powder, and milk. In a saucepan, heat to simmering the chicken stock, potatoes, carrots, apple juice, and chicken. Add about ¼ cup of the hot liquid to the egg yolk mixture, and stir to blend; add more liquid and blend again. Then slowly stir in the egg yolk mixture to the remaining hot stock mixture and cook over very low heat, stirring constantly, until it slightly thickens. Do not overcook and curdle the egg mixture. If both young and old are eating this, ladle out enough for the young and add a little extra apple juice to their portion. Add the sherry to the pot for adults. Season to taste with salt and pepper. Chill and serve.

Makes about 6 cups

It's handy to keep a bag of frozen potatoes in the freezer for this kind of dish.

Vegetable Bread Soup (in Tuscany called *Ribollita*)

Every cook makes bread soup a different way, but nearly all use stale bread, herbs, garlic, tomatoes, and assorted vegetables. My daughter-in-law makes a wonderful Tomato Bread Soup because she has an abundance of fresh tomatoes in her garden. I like to use leafy green vegetables because I usually get carried away at the farmers' market and forget I already have spinach or chard or kale in the refrigerator. Be sure and use a firm, dense bread such as an Italian loaf or a French bread or baguette — sandwich bread falls apart too quickly when it hits the broth. (Old bagels don't work, either, and I don't recommend stale English muffins.) In making this soup, use your imagination and substitute a bit. Following are three bread soups that can act as your guide to others.

1 garlic clove, minced
1 cup minced celery, carrots, and parsley mixture (this is called "odori")
4 tablespoons olive oil, plus extra at the table
1 large can (28 ounces) plum tomatoes, cut into chunks
2 medium potatoes, peeled and coarsely chopped
1 medium zucchini, thinly sliced
1 cup cauliflower florets, chopped
1 cup chopped cabbage, red or green
1 cup chopped Swiss chard
1 cup chopped spinach, fresh or frozen
1 can (15 ounces) white beans (like cannellini or Great Northern), drained
3 cups stale bread, cut in 1- to 1½-inch chunks

First, sauté the garlic and odori in the oil until soft. Add the tomatoes, potatoes, zucchini, cauliflower, cabbage, chard, and spinach; cook until all the vegetables are soft. Add the beans. Season with salt and freshly ground pepper to taste. Add the bread chunks, and set the soup aside to cool and let the flavors blend. (The soup can be refrigerated overnight at this point.) When ready to serve, return the soup pot to the stove and simmer for about 30 minutes. Serve with additional oil at the table. This delicious soup is just as good reheated the next day.

Makes about 3 quarts.

Vegetable Tomato Bread Soup I

Tomatoes are the vegetables here and in the following recipe. Though tomatoes are technically a fruit, they are usually used as a vegetable.

    3 cups coarsely cut up stale bread chunks
    1 quart rich chicken stock
    1 garlic clove, chopped and mashed
    4 tablespoons olive oil, plus extra at the table
    3 cups chopped very ripe fresh tomatoes (or 1 28-ounce can plum
        tomatoes)
    ¼ cup chopped fresh basil

First, soak the bread chunks in the stock and set aside. Next, sauté the garlic in oil over medium heat until slightly browned. Add the tomatoes, skin and all, and cook over high heat, stirring, until bubbly. Continue cooking on high for a few minutes, stirring to prevent sticking, until the tomatoes begin to thicken (the time will depend on whether fresh or canned ones are used). Add the basil and remove from heat. Remove the bread from stock and squeeze the bread over the tomato pot. Shred the bread and then add it to the pot along with the remaining stock. Season with black pepper to taste. Serve warm with additional olive oil at the table.

Makes 6 to 8 cups (depending on tomato juiciness)

Vegetable Tomato Bread Soup II

¼ cup olive oil
2 cloves garlic, minced
1 sweet onion, red or white, peeled and chopped
4 cups chopped very ripe fresh tomatoes
1 tablespoon fresh basil, minced
1 tablespoon fresh marjoram or oregano, minced
1 cup chicken stock
6 thick slices stale bread, cut into 1-inch chunks

In a heavy soup pot, heat the oil and sauté the garlic and onion until soft. Add the chopped tomatoes, herbs, and chicken stock. Season with salt and pepper to taste. Bring to a simmer and cook for about 10 minutes. Add the bread chunks and simmer for another 2 to 3 minutes. Remove from the heat and cool. Serve lukewarm.

Makes about 6 cups.

Any of these bread soups are good served with Abbie's Chicken Salad with Grapes.

Summer Fruit Soups

In the summer months, I drive back and forth to the Adirondack Mountains, passing through the Champlain Valley where the soil is rich, the days are warm, the air from the lakes and Hudson River is moist, and farmers' fields are loaded with strawberries, raspberries, and melons. The apple orchards are covered with delicate white and pink blossoms when I begin my treks in the spring, and by the time summer begins to wind down, truckloads of apples flank the highway and beckon drivers to stop. I, for one, can't resist, even though I have two old apple trees of my own — enough for picking one up from the ground whenever I walk the dogs and enough gnarly ones for making jelly and jam. But those roadside varieties are always perfectly round, red, and tempting — so I stop and buy a sack of them and eat one as I drive on.

As a result of these stops, I usually end up with too many of everything that's in season, so apples, along with the other fruits of summer, get used in soups as well as desserts.

Fruit soups make wonderful first courses. They are usually light and delicate and won't fill you up too much. They can be followed with a hot or cold dinner, whichever suits your fancy for the evening.

Apple Delight

While an apple a day may keep the doctor away, a cup of this soup on a late-summer day will bring good cheer and compliments. It can be served cold or at room temperature, but it's also good when served hot as a first course. Children and adults like it equally. Serving it with cold meat and Mustard Potato Salad with Sorrel will also make a hit.

2 pounds firm, juicy apples, cut up in chunks
2 small onions, chopped
2 tablespoons vegetable or olive oil
1 cup beef stock (or canned beef broth)
½ teaspoon Worcestershire sauce
thin lemon slices for garnish

Cook the apples in enough water to barely cover until they're soft. Extract the juice by dripping the apples through a jelly bag or cheesecloth (do not squeeze because that will make the juice cloudy). This should make about 2 cups of juice. In a saucepan, sauté the onions in oil until golden. Add the beef stock and Worcestershire sauce. Heat to simmering and cook for about 5 minutes. Add the apple juice. Season to taste with salt and pepper. Strain the soup to remove the onions. Reheat and serve, garnished with a thin slice of lemon in each cup.

Makes 6 half-cup servings

Cantaloupe

This can be a special preliminary to a summer dinner party featuring almost any grilled meat. The delectability of the soup will depend on the quality of the melon. Where I live in upstate New York, it's safest to serve this in August, when the local melons are ripe. A juicy Hand melon from Saratoga County in New York State is ideal.

I frequently pass by the Hand farm when I go back and forth to the Adirondack Mountains in the summer. Mr. Hand bred this particular melon many years ago, and now it is standard fare in the summer markets in many states. And what a treat!

In a literal sense, a "cantaloupe" only comes from that region in France where this particular muskmelon is grown. The ones in the U.S. are just plain muskmelons, but long ago they got to be known as cantaloupes, after their French cousins. Some of these melons have a rougher skin on the outside than others, but they all have the same orange flesh on the inside.

It's hard to pick the best and sweetest melon, and I prefer to leave it to the grower to tell me which one to buy. But as a general rule, if the stem end is a tad softer than the rest of the melon and has a sweet, melony smell, it is ripe and ready. Hard stem ends with no smell are doubtful.

1 very ripe sweet melon
1 cup chicken stock
1 cup milk
¼ cup sour cream
1 celery stalk (no leaves), minced
1 teaspoon minced thyme (fresh is best, but dried will do)
½ teaspoon ground cumin
1 tablespoon fresh lemon juice

Remove the seeds from the melon and scoop out the flesh. Puree in a blender or food processor with the remaining ingredients. Season to taste with a little salt and, if your melon is not as sweet as you would like, add a touch of sugar. Chill and serve very cold.

Makes about 4 cups

This makes a great summer supper if served with grilled meat and Rice Salad with Pine Nuts

Cherry Choice

Unusual — and delicious. A few cherries with stems alongside the soup cup on the plate make an attractive presentation.

1 pound fresh cherries, pitted and stems removed
1 cup dry red wine
2 cups chicken stock
1 strip lemon peel
1 cinnamon stick
1 teaspoon sugar
1 tablespoon cornstarch
½ cup water
sour cream or thin lemon slices for garnish

Combine the cherries, wine, chicken stock, lemon peel, cinnamon stick, and sugar in a saucepan. Bring the mixture to a boil, reduce heat, cover, and simmer for 15 minutes. Discard the lemon peel and cinnamon stick. Put the soup through a blender or food processor to puree, then return it to the saucepan. Mix the cornstarch with the water, stirring until smooth. Add it to the cherry puree. Cook the soup over very low heat, stirring constantly, for about 10 minutes or until slightly thickened. Cool. Season with salt to taste. Chill. Serve chilled, garnished with a dollop of sour cream or a thin lemon slice.

Makes 5-plus cups

For Jellied Cherry Choice, soften 1 envelope plain gelatin in ¼ cup water. Dissolve it in the soup while it is hot. Chill to serve.

Cold Blueberry

As this soup is fairly rich, serve only a small cupful. It's excellent on a hot August day, followed by a light meal of an omelet and mixed greens salad — plus maybe a cookie or two. It has red wine in it, but as the amounts are small, it should be all right for children, too. After all, the French give red wine to their young, and they seem to be healthy.

1 pint blueberries
2 cups water
2 tablespoons sugar
1 2-inch piece of cinnamon stick
½ lemon, sliced
½ cup dry red wine
1 cup sour cream
mint sprigs for garnish

Wash and drain the blueberries. Combine them in a saucepan with the water, sugar, cinnamon stick, and lemon slices. Mash the berries a bit with the back of a wooden spoon. Bring the mixture to a boil, reduce heat, mash the berries a bit more, and simmer for 20 to 30 minutes. Strain the mixture through a fine sieve into a bowl. Add the red wine. Chill. When cold, add the sour cream and blend well. Season to taste with salt. Serve cold, garnished with mint sprigs.

Makes about 5 cups.

Pretty color. Good, too.

Curried Apple Cream

According to *The Columbia Encyclopedia*, there are probably more than 7,500 varieties of apples, though only about 50 are used commercially. My tome is fairly old now, so there are probably many more than 50 available in markets around the world. With so many, it's no wonder cooks now use them in soups, salads, vegetable dishes, and desserts — to say nothing of snacks. What would a lunch box be without an apple! The following soup is good either hot or cold. It's a wonderful summer meal when served with Watercress and Chicken Salad and crusty bread, topped off with your favorite ice cream.

4 to 6 firm juicy apples, quartered
2 medium-size onions, chopped
1 celery stalk, chopped
2 tablespoons oil, olive or vegetable
1 cup chicken stock
juice of ½ lemon (no seeds)
½ cup plain yogurt
½ cup whole milk
1 teaspoon curry powder
1 teaspoon ground coriander

In a covered saucepan, cook the apples in about 1 inch of water until they are soft. When cooked, push them through a sieve or process in a food mill to get a soupy puree. Set aside. Sauté the onions and celery in oil until golden. Add the apple puree. Put the onion-celery-apple mix in a food processor to puree. Return to saucepan. Add the chicken stock, lemon juice, yogurt, milk, and spices and blend well. Bring to a simmer on low heat, stirring constantly. Cover and cook for about 20 minutes. Season with salt and pepper to taste. Either serve hot or chill and serve cold, stirring well just before serving.

Makes about 5 cups

Lemon Zip

Very little beats the flavor of lemon on a summer's day, whether a Popsicle, a sorbet, a pie, a drink, or a soup. I'm always glad to see that children still have lemonade stands at the edges of their lawns, just the way kids have done for many generations.

This soup is good for any outdoor meal — inside, too. Fresh herbs from the garden or window box are ideal garnishes. Try following it with Five Cs Salad (cabbage, celery, carrots, chives, and chicken).

    2 egg yolks
    juice of 2 fresh lemons
    1 tablespoon grated lemon zest
    2 cups chicken stock, heated
    ½ cup whole milk (or light cream)
    ½ cup plain yogurt
    fresh coarsely chopped parsley, chives, or mint leaves for garnish

Beat the egg yolks with the lemon juice and lemon zest. Gradually add about ¼ cup at a time of the hot stock to the egg mix, beating well after each addition. Then add the egg mix to the remainder of the stock in a saucepan. Over very low heat, stirring constantly, cook the soup until it slightly thickens. Stir in the milk and yogurt. Blend well and heat through, but do not let it boil or even simmer. Season with salt to taste. Serve hot, warm, or cold, garnished with fresh herbs.

Makes 6 ½-cup servings

Party Pineapple Ice

Just thinking about this soup cools a fevered brow and sets the tone for summer reveries. If you want to use this for the kids, too, substitute ginger ale for the sparkling wine. Teetotalers will like this idea, too.

1 fresh, sweet pineapple
1 ½ cups water
½ cup sugar
1 teaspoon ground ginger
½ cup pineapple juice
1 bottle (750 milliliters) dry sparkling wine (or ginger ale)

Peel and core the pineapple. Set aside the edible fruit and place the core in a saucepan with the water. Bring to a boil and simmer for about 15 minutes. Strain the softened core through a cheesecloth or fine sieve. Discard core pieces. Combine the pineapple-core juice with the sugar, ginger, and pineapple juice in a saucepan. Cover and bring to a simmer. Meanwhile, cut the edible pineapple flesh into small pieces. Combine this with the simmering juice and return to a simmer. Cover and let cook for about 20 minutes, or until the fruit is very soft. Cool and chill. When chilled, add the sparkling wine (or ginger ale), return to refrigerator for about 30 minutes, and then serve.

Makes about 10 servings.

Peachy Creamy

Georgia is known as the Peach State — and for good reason. Those ripe, golden-peach-colored globes are incomparable. When I was a child, my brother and I would seasonally indulge in that exquisite pleasure of biting into really ripe peaches, so succulent that the juice dribbled down our chins and slid down our bare forearms. As we were usually in bathing suits or something similar, it didn't matter — a good *whish* with the garden hose cleaned us right up. I'm sure peaches fresh off the tree and piled into bushel baskets still taste that good, but now I'm usually in long-sleeved gardening clothes, and somehow it's not quite the same. However, this soup is still as good as it ever was, using that sweet summer fruit.

> boiling water
> 5 or 6 large ripe peaches
> 1 tablespoon lemon juice
> ¼ cup sugar
> ½ cup water
> ¼ cup ginger ale
> ¼ cup dry white wine
> ½ cup light cream
> ½ cup sour cream
> mint sprigs for garnish

Peel peaches by briefly dipping them in boiling water to loosen skin. Pit and cut into quarters. Toss with lemon juice and set aside. Combine the sugar, water, and ginger ale in a saucepan and bring to a boil. Reduce the heat, add the peaches, cover, and simmer for about 5 minutes. Remove from the heat and cool. Puree the peach mixture in a blender or food processor. Combine with the cream and sour cream. Blend in the wine. (If the kids are eating this, too, ladle out enough peach mix for their portions and reduce the wine amount to about ⅓ cup for adults.) Chill. Garnish each serving with a mint sprig if desired.

Makes 6 or more cups.

This soup is good with Wilted Greens with Spicy Pork salad.

Plum Delicious

I used to have two plum trees that produced an incredible amount of juicy purple plums. There were so many, they hung from the trees like clusters of grapes. Not only did we eat them fresh from the tree, but I made lots of jam and plum pies and finally experimented with plum soup. It was such a hit, I made this soup over and over. Alas, the trees are no more, but I still make the soup — only now I have to buy the plums. Easy and delicious. (Canned plums work, too.)

4 cups plums, pitted and cut up
1 cup water
½ cup sugar
1 cup chicken stock
1 cup sour cream

Simmer the plums in the water and sugar until they are soft. Puree in a blender or food processor with the chicken stock and sour cream. Chill and eat. That's it.

Makes 7-plus cups.

This soup and Curried Lamb with Garden Peas Salad makes an unusual and delicious meal.

Raspberry Jell

This is a wonderful red color. If you don't need it while the raspberry season is in full swing, put some berries in the freezer and make it later. Try serving it with Minced Ham Salad.

1 pint raspberries
2 cups plus another ¼ cup water
½ lemon, seeded and sliced
2 tablespoons sugar
1 celery stalk, cut up (no greens)
1 package plain gelatin
sour cream for garnish

In a saucepan, combine the berries, 2 cups of water, lemon, sugar, and celery. Bring to a boil. Reduce the heat, cover, and simmer for 30 minutes. Strain through a cheesecloth bag or fine sieve — do not squeeze or push the mixture through the sieve as that will make the juice cloudy. Soften the gelatin in the ¼ cup of cold water. Add it to the raspberry soup and reheat to dissolve the gelatin. Season with salt to taste. Chill to jell. Serve with a dollop of sour cream in each cup.

Makes 5 to 6 cups

Rhubarb Roundup

Grownups and kids both will like this — and will be guessing what's in it. Good with Yellow Rice with Summer Squash and Pine Nuts salad.

2 onions, chopped
1 garlic clove, minced
1 tart apple, peeled, cored, and diced
2 tablespoons oil, olive or vegetable
4 cups young rhubarb, cut in 1/4-inch pieces
2 tablespoons flour
3 cups beef stock (or canned beef broth), heated
¼ cup sugar
1 cup whole milk
½ cup sherry

Sauté the onions, garlic, and apple in the oil until soft. Add the rhubarb. Sprinkle on the flour and mix well. Gradually stir in the beef stock and cook until slightly thickened. Then stir in the sugar. Bring to barely simmering and cook gently for 5 to 7 minutes, or until the rhubarb is soft and tender. Stir in the milk. If you want to remove some for the kids before adding the sherry, now is the time to do it. Add the sherry and season to taste with salt and pepper. Chill. Serve cold.

Makes almost 2 quarts.

Garden tip: If you want to keep your rhubarb plants producing all summer and into the fall, cut off the flower stalks that spring up in the center. (I try to catch them when they are in tight bud and use them in flower arrangements, along with some of the smaller leaves.)

Watermelon Ice

This is a real summer treat. It's delicious on a hot day, followed by a seafood salad, blueberry muffins, and brownies for dessert.

When I was growing up in the South, where watermelons covered whole fields, we were welcome to take one to eat with our hands. The trick is to split them open by dropping them from shoulder height onto the stem end. (I always let my older and taller brother do this.) The melon not only splits open, but the red flesh in the center falls away from the seeds that are nearer the rind. All we had to do was pick up the center pieces and eat them (getting a few seeds, but not too many). Of course, they were always warm from having been out in the sunny field, and somehow that made them taste all the sweeter. For the following soup, though, icy cold to the point of freezing is the way to go.

  3 cups ripe watermelon pieces (no seeds or rind)
  1 teaspoon grated onion
  1 tablespoon fresh lemon juice
  sprig of mint for garnish

Puree all ingredients in a blender or food processor. Spread mixture in a shallow pan and put in the freezer. Just as it gets to the mushy stage, mix thoroughly, using a whisk or eggbeater. Return the pan to the freezer to set a little more — do not let it freeze to a solid block. If it's freezing too fast, whip it some more and refrigerate for a short time, and then return the pan to the freezer. It should be the consistency of sorbet or soft sherbet. Serve at once, garnished with a sprig of mint.

Makes 6 cups.

Market & Garden
Vegetable Soups

Farmers' markets have sprung up in parking lots and abandoned fields across America, and they are nearly always wonderful. Sellers sit in canvas director's chairs behind a makeshift table surrounded by bushel baskets of produce, anything from green beans to zucchini. The vegetables are fresh, succulent, and well priced. I can hardly drive past one without stopping, even if just to look and have a few words with the farmers.

If you have your own vegetable garden, you know what pleasure and pride come with picking those early sweet peas, snapping off the first small summer squashes, even having to find recipients for the overflow of cucumbers and zucchini.

It doesn't matter if you have a large garden or a small one, the reward is always great. One of my sons and his family live in a large city with a small yard big enough for the kids' swing set and the dog, yet manage to reserve a plot less than the size of a parking space for herbs and vegetables — and what abundance they get! It puts me to shame with all the area I have for growing. So size is irrelevant. Desire and pleasure are the prime factors.

But don't forget the farmer who brings his own specialties to your neighborhood. Your own garden is great, but those farmers have really green thumbs.

Asparagus and Lemon Soup with Orzo

The minute we get into spring, I start to think about fresh local asparagus. There's nothing like it. Fortunately for me, my neighbor down the road usually has more than she can eat or wants to freeze, and knowing how I love those fresh stalks, she gives me a call. I also know all the farmers who grow it for sale, and I'm always a ready customer. Freshly picked, it is one of the treats of spring and early summer. The following soup is as delicious as a warm June day — and good with Simple Salad of Greens and Toms.

> 2 quarts chicken stock
> ½ cup dried orzo
> 1 pound fresh asparagus (tough stems snapped off), broken into
>   1-inch pieces
> 2 eggs
> ½ cup finely chopped scallions
> ¼ cup fresh lemon juice

In a large pot, bring the chicken stock to a medium boil. Add the orzo, and cook for about 10 minutes. While the stock is still slightly boiling, add the asparagus pieces and cook another 5 minutes. Meanwhile, whisk the eggs in a small bowl. Lift out about ¼ cup of the boiling chicken stock and stir into the eggs; blend well. Repeat. Then add the egg mixture to the cooking pot, reduce the heat, and cook while stirring constantly until slightly thickened and just a little creamy. Remove from the heat and stir in the scallions and lemon juice. Season with salt and pepper to taste. Serve hot, warm, or cold.

Makes 10 or more cups.

Basil-Tomato Medley

Many varieties of basil can be found in the markets nowadays, but I continue to grow the old-fashioned common green one. However, there's no reason to think any of them wouldn't be good in this soup. Use really ripe and sweet red tomatoes.

3 tablespoons olive oil
1 garlic clove, minced
1 small onion, minced
1 stalk celery, including greens, minced
½ green pepper, seeded and minced
4 or 5 large ripe tomatoes, peeled and chopped
1 cup minced fresh basil
½ teaspoon sugar
2 cups chicken stock
croutons
basil leaves for garnish

In the olive oil in a large pot, sauté the garlic, onion, celery, and green pepper until soft. Add the tomatoes, basil, sugar, and chicken stock. Bring to a simmer and cook uncovered for about 30 minutes. Remove from the heat, season with salt and pepper to taste, cool, and serve with a few croutons in each cup plus a basil leaf for garnish. Serve cool or chilled.

Makes 6 cups.

Note: If you want a thinner soup, add some tomato juice.

Beets and Beet Greens

Fresh-from-the-garden beets and beet greens are among the great summer treats. This is an easy recipe, and it's really delicious. Try serving it with Mimi's Warm Potato Salad and cold meat for a tasty summer meal.

> 6 small beets, scrubbed clean (tails and tops removed if using beets other than those that come with the greens)
> 4 cups chopped beet greens
> 1 cup reserved beet cooking liquid
> 1 garlic clove, minced
> 1 tablespoon olive oil
> 2 cups beef stock (or canned beef broth)
> ½ cup sour cream

Cover the beets with water and simmer, covered, until soft. Save 1 cup of the cooking liquid.

When cool, slip the skins from the beets and discard. Cut up the beets into chunks. In a blender or food processor, puree the beet chunks with the cup of cooking liquid. Set aside. Meanwhile, in a large pot, sauté the garlic in the oil until soft. Add the pureed beets. Then add the beet greens and beef stock and bring to a simmer. Cook for at least 10 minutes, or until the greens and stems are soft. Blend in the sour cream. Season to taste with salt. Serve hot, lukewarm, or cold.

Makes 5 or 6 cups.

Broccoli with Broccoli Rabe

This is a wonderful green color. If the little ones will object to the broccoli rabe floating around in the soup, ladle out enough for their portions before adding the chopped rabe. Good with Mustard Potato Salad.

    2 tablespoons oil, olive or vegetable
    1 large leek, washed and chopped
    1 bunch broccoli (1 pound or a little more), tough end of stalk
        removed, stalks and florets chopped
    2 ½ cups chicken stock
    ½ cup evaporated milk
    3 or 4 stalks broccoli rabe, ends trimmed off, leafy part chopped
    ½ cup sour cream

Heat the oil in large, heavy pot. Add the leek and sauté until soft. Add the broccoli, chicken stock, and milk. Bring to a simmer, cover, and simmer for about 20 minutes. Puree the soup in 3 or 4 batches in a blender or food processor. Return the puree to the pot and bring it to a medium boil. Add the chopped broccoli rabe and cook for about 5 minutes. Stir in the sour cream and season with salt to taste. Serve hot, lukewarm, or cold.

Makes about 6 cups.

Carrots 'n Cream Concoction

My very first stab at growing my own vegetables was somewhat less than successful. The lettuce came out all right, and so did a row of potatoes. Everything else sent me back to the drawing board, especially the carrots. I had envisioned champion carrots, the kind with lacy green tops and long orange bottoms that Bugs Bunny would covet. Friends as well as seed catalogues had assured me they were very easy to grow. But I planted the seeds much too close together, and, of course, the result was pitiful, the little gnarly things stunted and twisted around each other like nestling corkscrews. Now I know better, and fresh carrots, whether from a backyard garden or the farmer's market, are supremely sweet, crunchy, and delicious.

In this carrot soup, I use the outer stalks of celery, saving the tender inner stalks for nibbles. The other ingredients may sound strange, but once blended with the carrots their individual tastes disappear and simply add to the delicious whole. This is a really nice summer treat that all ages will like. Try it with Grab-bag Rice and Peas Salad.

3 cups chicken stock (or vegetable or beef stock — I prefer chicken)
5 medium-sized carrots, scraped and cut up
2 celery stalks, cut up (outside stringy part removed)
1 tablespoon chopped fresh basil
1 teaspoon olive oil
½ large banana (or 1 small one)
½ cup cottage cheese
⅔ cup sour cream
1 teaspoon curry powder

In a large pot, combine the chicken stock, carrots, celery, basil, and oil. Bring to a boil, reduce the heat, cover, and simmer for about 15 minutes, or until the carrots and celery are soft.

In a blender or food processor, coarsely puree the mixture so that vegetables will have some minced texture. Return to the pot. In the same blender or processor, add the banana, cottage cheese, sour cream, and curry powder. Puree until smooth. Stir into the carrot mixture. Season with salt to taste. This soup is best served slightly warm or at room temperature — though cold is OK.

Makes about 6 cups.

Carrot-Ginger Bisque

This wonderful creamy soup is a perfect first course. Followed by Curried Lamb with Garden Peas Salad and blueberry muffins, it makes an ideal summer meal.

    3 tablespoons oil
    1 clove garlic, minced
    5 large carrots, scraped and cut up plus 1 carrot for garnish
    1 sweet onion, chopped
    1 potato, peeled and chopped
    4 cups chicken stock
    2 cups milk, whole or low-fat
    ½ cup ricotta cheese
    1 tablespoon ground ginger
    carrot curls and/or grated fresh ginger for garnish

In a large pot, heat the oil and sauté the garlic, onions, carrots, and potato. When the vegetables are soft, add the chicken stock and bring to a boil. Reduce the heat, cover, and simmer for about 30 minutes to really blend the flavors. Puree in a blender or food processor in small batches with the milk and ricotta and the ginger. Season with salt to taste. Serve cold. Sliver carrot curls with a vegetable peeler from a scraped carrot for garnish. Grate the fresh ginger — use sparingly. I like to use both for grown-ups, carrots only for kids.

Makes 8 or more cups.

Casual Cabbage and Tomato

My sons liked raw vegetables when they were quite young. In fact, they preferred most green, yellow, or orange vegetables — colors that just about covered most of the garden — served raw rather than cooked. This soup is crispy, cold, crunchy, and casual — namely, easy. Whether the little ones in your house will eat it or not depends on their attitude toward raw veggies. I'm sure grown-ups will like it. Try serving it with assorted crackers, cheeses, and fruit. Umm, umm good — and just the ticket when you'd prefer to be outside in the sun instead of in the kitchen.

½ small green cabbage, finely chopped (2 generous cups)
1 medium sweet white onion, such as a Vidalia
1 celery stalk, including some of the leafy top, finely chopped
½ sweet green pepper, seeded and finely chopped
2 canned pimentos, finely chopped
5 large ripe tomatoes, peeled and chopped
1 teaspoon poppy seeds
1 cup sour cream

Mix all the ingredients together. Season to taste with salt and pepper. Serve cold.

Serves 8.

Good with Minced Ham Salad.

Cauliflower Plus

If the queen were coming to dine, I would serve her cauliflower — any queen, any meal. It's beautiful to behold, easy to cook in a variety of ways, and always tasty. Here's a rich, hearty soup that will appeal to all ages. It's good with Marinated Steak and Chard Salad.

2 tablespoons oil
1 onion, chopped
1 garlic clove, minced
2 tablespoons flour
1 cup hot chicken stock
1 cup milk, heated
1 potato, peeled and sliced very thin
2 cups cauliflower florets, cut up
½ cup each plain yogurt and half-and-half cream
1 teaspoon ground cumin
1 teaspoon grated horseradish
1 cup green beans, ends cut off and pods finely chopped, steamed
    until al dente
minced parsley or chives for garnish

In a large heavy pot, heat the oil, and sauté the garlic and onion until they are soft. Sprinkle on the flour and mix well. Gradually add the hot stock and the hot milk, stirring constantly, to make a thin, creamy soup base. (If too thick, add more milk.) Add the potato and cauliflower, cover the pot, reduce the heat to barely simmering, and cook until the potato and cauliflower are soft. Remove from the heat. Stir in the yogurt, cream, cumin, and horseradish. Puree in batches in a blender or food processor. Season to taste with salt and pepper.

Lest you think I've forgotten the green beans, now is the time to add them, mixing them thoroughly into the soup. The slightly crunchy taste of green beans in the creamy white soup is a nice contrast. Top each bowl with some more greenery, either parsley or chives — remembering that little ones often don't like floating green bits in their soup.

Makes 6-plus cups.

If you prefer a completely white soup, omit the green beans and the garnish.

Celery and Asparagus with Peas

Celery might be year-round, but asparagus is not, so I consider this to be a spring and early summer soup. Fresh green peas are great in this soup, but frozen ones can be used. These three flavors comingle very nicely. The first time I served this recipe, I worried a bit about the combination, but a friend who is a terrific cook mumbled, "What clever things to put together." So I relaxed. I think you'll like serving this, too. I have yet to find a child who won't eat it, so dish it up for all ages.

  2 cups chicken stock
  1 large bunch celery, tops included, washed and cut into small
    pieces
  ¼ cup thinly sliced scallions
  1 medium potato, peeled and cubed
  1 ½ cups fresh peas or 1 package (10 ounces) frozen
  1 pound asparagus, tough ends discarded and stalks cut into 1/2-
    inch pieces
  1 cup plain yogurt
  1 cup sour cream

Cook the celery, scallions, and potatoes in simmering chicken stock, covered, until the vegetables are barely tender. Add the peas and asparagus, and cook for another few minutes, until tender. Stir in the yogurt and sour cream. Season with salt to taste. Serve at room temperature or cold.

Makes 8 to 10 cups.

Creamy Corn Chowder

There's a farm not too far from me, in Lanesboro, Massachusetts, that grows only corn and starts selling it in late summer from a roadside stand. Over the past several years I have continued to buy the old favorites such as Silver Queen and Butter-and-Sugar as well as anything new that was offered. Last year the farm introduced a new triple-sweet corn that was worth every extra penny it cost. It was the kind of taste you dream about during the long winter months.

I always buy and cook more than I need for dinner and have a wonderful time creating new dishes with the leftovers. The following chowder is easy and sure to please adults and kids alike. Look in the salad section of this book for more ways to use corn leftovers — though if you get the new triple-sweet variety you may not *have* leftovers.

    2 bacon strips
    1 medium onion, chopped
    1 potato, peeled and chopped
    1 sweet red pepper, seeded and finely chopped
    2 tablespoons flour
    ½ teaspoon dry mustard
    1 can evaporated milk (or half-and-half), heated
    4 or 5 ears of cooked corn, kernels removed and cobs scraped to get
        all the sugary liquid
    1 cup plain yogurt

Cook the bacon until crisp; remove, crumble, and set aside. In the bacon drippings, sauté the onion, potato, and red pepper until they are soft. Sprinkle on the flour and mustard and mix well. Gradually add the heated milk (or cream), stirring constantly to thicken. Stir in the corn and yogurt. Add the crumbled bacon. Season to taste with salt and pepper. Serve hot or warm.

Makes 8 or 9 cups.

Note: Chilled Cream of Corn Soup is excellent, too. For that, omit the red pepper and bacon. Before adding the corn, puree the cooked onion, potato, cream, flour, and mustard in a blender or food processor. Stir in the yogurt. Add the corn, season to taste with salt and pepper, and chill.

Cucumber and Yogurt

If you have any cucumbers at all in your home vegetable garden, chances are you'll have too many of them. One year we were away during the crucial week at the height of the cucumber-producing season, and when we returned home — after only a few days, mind you — we had to take the large wheelbarrow to the garden to gather the cukes. We not only made cucumber relish, but we peeled and sliced them for the freezer to use during the fall and winter months, and we ate them in soups, sandwiches, salads, and vegetable dishes (scalloped cucumbers are delicious). The following is an easy recipe that's mighty tasty on a hot day. It's of Middle Eastern origin. My grandchildren like it, even the fussy ones.

2 cups finely chopped cucumbers, peeled and seeded
2 cups plain yogurt
1 cup milk
1 garlic clove, finely minced
2 tablespoons minced curly parsley
½ cup golden raisins, completely separated
½ cup pine nuts
1 teaspoon good white vinegar (*not* red-wine vinegar)
1 teaspoon sugar

Mix all the ingredients together, and chill. Stir well before serving so that the raisins and pine nuts won't be sitting on the bottom. Good with Red Rice salad.

Makes 6 cups

Curious Red Vegetable Soup

There's really nothing curious about all these ingredients turning red — I just like the name, and it appeals to kids. If they should question what's in this soup, hedge and tell them it's one that Curious George would like.

I like growing both beets and beet greens in the garden — and so do most farmers. There shouldn't be any problem finding some wonderful sweet beets in any roadside stand during the mid- to late-summer season.

2 cups tomato juice
2 cups finely diced cooked and peeled beets
2 hard-boiled eggs, chopped
1 celery stalk, chopped
1 small cucumber, peeled, seeded, and chopped
2 cups diced potatoes, cooked and peeled
1 sweet onion, minced
½ cup buttermilk
½ cup plain yogurt
2 tablespoons lemon juice
¼ cup minced chives
1 garlic clove, minced
1 teaspoon minced dillweed

Combine all the ingredients. Season to taste. Chill.

Makes about 2 quarts

Curried Cucumber and Grape Soup

Cucumbers, being fairly bland, seem to lend themselves to most spices and herbs. Try this combination. The main ingredients should be green or white — nice colors for summer.

2 medium cucumbers, peeled, seeded, and finely chopped
3 tablespoons rice vinegar (or white wine vinegar)
2 cups chicken stock (or vegetable stock if serving vegetarians)
1 avocado, peeled, pitted, and minced
1 cup white grapes, minced
1 cup sour cream
¼ cup dry Vermouth or dry white wine
¼ cup minced watercress (parsley is a good substitute)
1 tablespoon curry powder
1 teaspoon white pepper

Mix all the ingredients in a large pot. Simmer briefly for about 10 minutes to allow the flavors to blend. Cool and then refrigerate. The curry powder will be the only nongreen or white color, and it will disappear — the color, not the flavor. Try this with Stir-fried Beef and Peppers salad.

Makes 8 or so cups.

Curried Lime-Pea Soup

Don't worry about this being too sweet. It has a refreshing taste that kids and grown-ups alike will enjoy. We like it with a pasta salad such as Twists and Cukes.

    1 medium onion, chopped
    1 garlic clove, cut up
    2 tablespoons oil, olive or vegetable
    2 cups shelled fresh peas (or frozen)
    2 cups chicken stock
    1 cup plain yogurt
    1 teaspoon ground cumin seed
    1 tablespoon curry powder
    1 packet lime Jello
    ½ cup boiling water
    lime slices for garnish

Sauté the onion and garlic in the oil until soft. Add the peas and chicken stock, bring to a simmer, and cook for about 5 minutes, or until the peas are done. Remove from the heat and puree in a food processor or blender. Put the pureed soup in a large bowl and add the yogurt, cumin seed, and curry powder. Stir to thoroughly blend.

Meanwhile, completely dissolve the lime Jello in the boiling water, then stir it into the soup. Cover and refrigerate to chill. When ready to serve, stir thoroughly, and garnish with a slice of lime. Kids usually like this touch.

Makes about 6 cups.

Dandy Green Soup

I have always liked the early greens that pop up in the spring, especially dandelion greens and chives. Dandelion greens that grow in shady or dappled-sun areas are the most tender. Many growers cultivate them in vegetable gardens, but I have always relied on the ones that grow wild at the edge of my woods or in surprise places around the house. Try to pick them before the flower stalk appears — the same with chives. They are both good in salads, pasta dishes, and soups. This may be one recipe that kids won't name as a favorite, but it's worth a try. Good with Turkey and Chickpeas salad.

    3 tablespoons olive oil
    1 garlic clove, minced
    1 potato, peeled and cubed
    1 tablespoon flour
    2 cups chicken stock, heated
    8 cups finely chopped dandelion greens
    1 teaspoon ground mace
    ½ cup finely cut chives
    1 cup half-and-half cream

Heat the oil, and sauté the garlic and potato over low heat until they're soft. Sprinkle the flour over all and evenly mix in. Gradually add the chicken stock, stirring, and cook until slightly thickened. Add the dandelion greens and mace, pushing them down in the liquid, and bring the soup to a simmer. Cover and cook until the greens are quite wilted and soft. Stir in the half-and-half and chives. Season with salt to taste. Serve warm, at room temperature, or chilled.

If you prefer, the entire pot of soup can be put through a blender or food processor to puree. Either way—chunky or pureed — it's good .

Makes 6 or more cups.

Dilly Delight

Fresh dill straight from the garden provides a strong, aromatic flavor that is truly unique. However, it's possible that it's too much for little ones, so you might want to ladle out enough soup for them before adding the dill. But if you've got food-adventurous kids, go for it.

1 leek, thoroughly washed and cut up
1 small potato, peeled and cut up
2 tablespoons oil, olive or vegetable
4 cups cut-up or sliced zucchini
2 cups chicken stock
1 cup whole milk
1 cup sour cream
¼ cup minced fresh dillweed, plus additional sprigs for garnish

Sauté the leek and potato in the oil until they're soft. Add the zucchini and chicken stock and bring to a boil. Reduce the heat to simmer, cover, and cook until the zucchini is tender. Puree the soup in a blender or food processor. Pour into a large bowl and add the milk and sour cream. Season to taste with salt. Ladle out enough soup for the little ones; to the remainder, add the minced dill. Chill. Garnish with dill sprigs.

Makes about 8 cups.

Fresh Fields Galore

This wonderful soup uses lots of different summer vegetables as well as some meat and dried beans. It's hearty and a favorite in my house for both big and little people. Great with corn bread.

2 tablespoons oil, vegetable or olive
1 pound ground turkey
1 small onion, chopped
1 garlic clove, minced
3 cups chicken stock
1 potato, peeled and diced
1 cup green beans, cut up
1 summer squash, diced
2 carrots, scraped and cut up
2 or more tablespoons fresh marjoram, summer savory, basil, or
    other herbs
1 can (15-ounces) Great Northern or cannellini beans, drained and
    rinsed
¼ cup sherry or apple juice

Heat the oil and lightly brown the turkey, onion, and garlic. Add all the remaining ingredients, except the sherry or apple juice. Reduce the heat, cover, and simmer for about 20 minutes or until the vegetables are soft. Divide the soup into two pots and add the sherry to the pot for adults and the apple juice to the one for kids. Serve hot or warm.

Makes about 2 ½ quarts.

Margot's Gazpacho

Our late aunt, Margot Whitney Beardsley, was one of the great cooks. In our family it was said that she could take day-old roadkill and make it taste superb. She was in a four-person group of cooks who got together once a month to cook and eat — and James Beard was another one of the four. I once met him at a cooking demonstration/lecture; I went backstage to introduce myself and tell him I was Margot's niece. The next day she called me to say "Jim" had just called her to say how nice it was of me to make the effort to come speak to him. He surely knew the thrill and honor were all mine, yet he made it clear to Aunt Margot that the pleasure had been his.

Margot, as is true of many great creative cooks, didn't like to divulge her secrets (or if these great creative cooks give you a recipe, there's always the nagging worry that a key ingredient has been left out). One year she asked me what I'd like for my birthday, and without a moment's hesitation I answered that I'd like her recipe for gazpacho. So here it is, and I hope up there in the Big Culinary Place in the Sky she won't mind that I'm sharing it with you. And if she left out a key ingredient, none of us will ever know — it tastes just like it should: light, crisp, slightly crunchy, and truly delicious.

1 garlic clove, minced
1 small onion, chopped
1 cucumber, peeled, seeded, and sliced
1 sweet green pepper, seeded and sliced
4 large ripe tomatoes, peeled and quartered
1 teaspoon salt
½ teaspoon freshly ground black pepper
¼ cup wine vinegar
¼ cup olive oil
½ cup tomato juice

Combine all the ingredients. Briefly put the mixture through a food processor or blender, about one-quarter at a time, to mince thoroughly but not puree. Season to taste if more salt is desired. Serve chilled.

Makes about 8 cups.

This is good with Ground Lamb and Black Beans salad.

Picnic Soup

This is when you raid the garden, plus add a few store items. Not much else is needed for a picnic, though some fruit and cookies might be a nice addition. Simple and tasty.

2 cups chicken stock
1 cup green beans, cut into ½-inch pieces
1 large potato, peeled and cubed
2 or 3 carrots, scraped and cut into small pieces
1 medium zucchini or yellow summer squash, cut into small pieces
1 celery stalk, cut up
1 medium cucumber, peeled, seeded, and cut up
1 firm apple, peeled, cored, and cut up
2 tablespoons chopped herbs, such as basil, marjoram, or savory — all of them or one
1 tablespoon minced chives
1 avocado, peeled, pitted, and cut into small cubes
1 cup diced cooked ham

To the chicken stock, add all the ingredients except the avocado and ham and cook everything (covered) until the vegetables are just soft. Remove from the heat, cool, and add the avocado and ham. Season to taste with salt and pepper. Voilà!

Makes 9 or 10 cups.

Tomato Yum-Yum

There's no such thing as too many tomatoes in the garden. Try this recipe for your red beauties.

3 ripe tomatoes, peeled and cubed
1 cucumber, peeled, seeded, and chopped
1 sweet onion, minced
1 ripe cantaloupe or honeydew melon, seeded and cubed
3 tablespoons minced fresh mint
1 cup plain yogurt
2 teaspoons curry powder
½ cup chicken stock

Mix all the ingredients. Season to taste with salt. Chill and serve. This soup is great for lunch served with some hot bread, or it's wonderful as a first course followed by Shrimp with Spinach and Bean Sprouts salad.

Makes 7 or 8 cups.

Vegetable Bisque

This is another recipe that uses lots of vegetables from the garden. Kids and adults both like it.

2 tablespoons butter or margarine
1 onion, chopped
1 carrot, sliced
1 celery stalk with leaves, diced
1 medium zucchini, diced
2 tablespoons flour
½ teaspoon chili powder
½ teaspoon savory
2 cups chicken stock, heated
4 large ripe tomatoes, peeled and chopped
¼ cup sherry (for adults)
thin lemon slices for garnish

Melt the butter in a large saucepan and add the onion, carrot, celery, and zucchini. Sauté the vegetables over low heat until they're soft. Sprinkle on the flour and mix well. Stir in the chili powder and savory. Gradually add the hot chicken stock, stirring constantly, and cook until the mixture is slightly thickened. Add the tomatoes. Then puree the soup in a food processor or blender. Ladle out enough for the kids' portions and then add the sherry to the remainder for the adults. Serve warm. Garnish the adults' servings with lemon slices.

Makes 8 or so cups.

Soups from the Sea & Other Waters

During the summer, when I visit my cousins on the coast of Maine, I always hope to get something from the sea at least one meal of every day I'm there — and duplications are no problem. We eat handpicked (and picked-over) crab at their wonderful old farmhouse that sits high on a point overlooking Penobscot Bay; or we drive to Blue Hill and have seafood salads at the terrific main-street restaurant that looks out over the harbor; or we zip across the water to Castine for lobster and haddock chowder. Somewhere along the way I usually manage to get in some scallops and striped bass. Pretty good eating.

If a trip to Maine is not part of your summer schedule, don't hesitate to go to your local market for wonderful fresh seafood and fish. The following recipes also use garden vegetables, making these tastes of the season especially nice for spring and summer dining.

Cucumbers and Salmon

Cucumbers are so easy to grow and so versatile, though they tend to take up a lot of room in the garden. One successful plant will provide the average home garden with enough cukes for the growing season. If they are to be frozen and used during the winter months in soups and stews, put in as many plants as you can find the space for. (To freeze, peel and cut them in strips or thick slices and freeze them on a cookie sheet. When frozen, package up as many as you think you'll need for a recipe, usually about two cups. Peeled, sliced in long strips, and sautéed in oil or butter, they make a wonderful year-round vegetable dish and are especially good with meat.)

Pickling cucumbers are a different matter and should not to be confused with the sweet eating variety.

> 1 pound fresh salmon, boned and skinned (canned may be used in
>   a pinch)
> ½ cup water
> 2 medium-size cucumbers, peeled, seeded, and sliced
> 1 tablespoon oil, olive or vegetable
> 1 teaspoon salt
> 1 large potato, peeled and chopped
> 1 cup chicken stock
> 1 cup whole milk
> ¼ teaspoon mace

Gently poach the salmon in the water in a covered pot for about 15 minutes or until flaky. Lift out the fish and set aside. To the cooking water, add the cucumbers, oil, salt, potato, and chicken stock. Simmer covered for about 15 minutes, or until the vegetables are soft. Stir in the milk and mace. Coarsely mince the mixture in a food processor or blender, and return it to the pot. Add the flaked salmon. Season with salt and pepper to taste. Serve warm or cold.

Makes about 8 cups.

This is good with any of the fruit salads.

Cukes with Fresh Herbs and Shrimp

Another cucumber recipe, simple and tasty. All ages should like it — even the young ones. One of the Simple Salads, such as Greens with Apples and Feta, is good with this soup.

2 or 3 cucumbers, peeled, large seeds removed, and chopped
2 cups chicken stock
1 teaspoon minced cilantro
2 teaspoons minced chervil
1 tablespoon minced chives
1 cup whole milk
1 slice white bread, crusts removed, cubed
1 cup shrimp, heads and tails removed and deveined

Combine all the ingredients except the shrimp in a pot and bring to a simmer. Cover and cook for about 15 to 20 minutes (longer won't hurt), or until the cucumbers are soft. Add the shrimp, return the soup to simmer, and cook until the shrimp turn pink, about 7 or 8 minutes. Coarsely mince everything in food processor or blender. Serve warm or cold.

Makes about 6 cups.

Friday Night Fish and Greens

Not too many years ago, it was a widespread custom to eat fish on Friday. While this was based on the religious beliefs of certain churches, the practice became accepted by a larger nonsectarian population. The following recipe is a result of those old customs. Instead of a meal of fish, potatoes, and a leafy green vegetable, this soup is a meal in one pot. If the little ones in your house don't like green things floating around in the soup bowl, use two pots.

2 pounds boned fish fillets (any non-oily variety)
1 quart water
2 sweet onions, chopped
2 bay leaves
1 teaspoon finely ground black pepper
6 cups packed fresh green leaves, such as spinach (or use 1 package frozen chopped)
1 young tender unpeeled cucumber, seeded and chopped
2 cups diced peeled potatoes (if using thin-skinned new potatoes, do not peel)
½ teaspoon nutmeg
½ cup dry white wine (apple juice for kids)
½ cup whole milk

Combine the fish, water, onions, bay leaves, and pepper in a large pot and bring to a boil. Reduce the heat and simmer for about 30 minutes. The fish will be thoroughly cooked and already flaking, but the time is needed to get the rich stock. If the fish has not flaked, lift it out and flake it with a fork and then return it to the pot. If the kids won't eat green things, divide the soup into two pots at this point. Add the greens to the soup for adults. Divide and add the cucumbers, potatoes, and nutmeg to both pots. Cook for another 15 minutes, or until vegetables are very soft.

To the pot for adults, add the wine; to the pot for the kids, add the apple juice. Add the milk to both pots proportionately. Lift out the bay leaves if you can find them.

Season with salt and pepper to taste. Serve piping hot — no matter how hot the day is.

Makes about 3 quarts.

Seafood Medley Supreme

This is a sort of Jambalaya and a great recipe for using your imagination. Add fish, ham, vegetables — whatever you fancy. The following is a basic guide. Little ones like it as much as adults do.

3 bacon slices, diced
1 onion, diced
1 stalk celery, chopped
¼ cup minced parsley
1 green pepper, seeded and chopped
3 cups tomatoes, juicy fresh ones or canned
½ cup clam juice, bottled or canned
1 teaspoon chili powder
dash cayenne pepper
chicken stock if needed
2 cups cooked shrimp, cut in pieces
½ pound haddock, boned
1 cup scallops, rinsed
2 or 3 cups hot cooked rice

Sauté the bacon, onion, celery, parsley, and green pepper in a large heavy pot until the vegetables are soft. Add the tomatoes, clam juice, chili powder, and cayenne. Bring to a simmer, cover, and cook over very low heat for about 30 minutes. If more liquid is needed to make a soupy base, add some chicken stock, ¼ cup at a time — don't let it get too liquidy. Add the shrimp, haddock, and scallops. Bring to a simmer, cover, and cook until the haddock is flaky and the scallops are tender. Season to taste with salt and pepper. Serve over hot cooked rice.

Makes about 3 quarts.

This is a meal in itself.

Shrimp Wiggle Soup

Shrimp Wiggle is the name of an entree found in old standard cookbooks. As a soup, it is superb either for a first course or a whole meal when served with some hot yeast rolls and a tasty salad — Wild Rice with Figs and Nuts would be a good choice. The soup is especially delicious when made in early summer with fresh garden peas. However, frozen peas work well, so don't hesitate to make this later in the season.

Incidentally, kids will like the name as well as the soup. The origin of the name? Your guess is as good as mine.

1 cup chicken stock, or canned chicken broth
1 cup peas, fresh or frozen
1 cup shrimp, heads and tails removed and deveined, and cut in half (if really large, cut up some more)
2 tablespoons butter or margarine
2 tablespoons flour
1 cup half-and-half cream, heated
1 cup whole milk, heated
1 teaspoon mace
1 teaspoon minced basil

Bring the chicken stock to a boil. Add the peas and shrimp, lower heat to simmer, cover, and cook for about 5 minutes, or until the shrimp are pink. Set the saucepan aside. In a separate pan, melt the butter, sprinkle on the flour, and stir to make a roux. Then gradually stir in the cream and milk, stirring constantly to slightly thicken and make a smooth, thin sauce. Stir in the mace and basil. Add the contents of the peas-and-shrimp mixture to the cream and milk mixture. Season to taste with salt and pepper. Serve warm or hot.

Makes 5 cups.

Spring Shad

In the early spring, it's always a joy to see the shadbush begin to bloom, for that's the sign that the shad are running in the rivers. The roe is always in great demand at fish markets, but many people overlook the rest of the fish. I like to get the whole fish: roe, bones, and all. I always ask someone at the market to fillet the fish for me, as shad is a really bony fish — lots of tiny, thin bones — and the experts do a much better job than I do. The fillets become one meal, as does the roe. Then this delicious soup is made from the bones, which still have a thin layer of flesh on both sides as the fish can't be filleted all the way to the backbone.

bones from 1 shad, cut into chunky sections
2 cups chicken stock
1 onion, sliced
1 celery stalk, cut up
1 lemon slice
4 or 5 whole cloves
2 parsley sprigs
¼ teaspoon peppercorns
1 bay leaf
1 tablespoon butter
1 tablespoon flour
½ cup sour cream
1 cup whole milk (or more if a thinner soup is desired)

In a large heavy pot, combine the fish bones, chicken stock, onion, celery, lemon, cloves, parsley, peppercorns, and bay leaf. Bring to a boil, reduce heat, cover, and simmer for 45 minutes. Strain through a fine sieve. Keep hot. Melt the butter and stir in the flour to make a roux. Gradually add the hot fish stock and cook, stirring constantly, until it slightly thickens. Add the milk. Season to taste with salt and pepper. Serve hot.

If you want an elegant soup, use some cooked roe as a garnish. Poach roe, separate eggs, toss with lemon juice, and add to each cup. Very fancy.

Makes about 6 cups.

This soup is good with one of the Fruit Salads like Pineapple, Cukes, and Ham, or one of the White Salad potato salads like Leek and Potato Salad.

Zucchini, Beans, and Cod Chowder

If you can't get cod, use another firm-flesh fish, such as haddock. Yellow crookneck squash may be substituted for the zucchini.

1 pound cod, boned
1 cup water
2 bacon slices, cut up
1 garlic clove, minced
1 onion, chopped
2 medium zucchini, chopped
1 cup cubed peeled potatoes
1 cup cooked white beans, such as Great Northern or garbanzo
1 cup half-and-half cream
¾ cup whole milk

Poach the cod in the water for about 10 minutes, or until it flakes easily. Flake the cod with a fork, and leave in the cooking water. In a large pan, lightly brown the bacon and then add the garlic, onion, zucchini, and potatoes. Cook over a low heat until the vegetables are soft. Add the cod and its cooking water to the vegetables. Stir in the beans, cream, and milk. Season to taste with salt and pepper. Serve warm or hot.

Makes about 2 ½ quarts.

Soups with Chicken & Other Meats

I n my family we eat more chicken and fish than other meats
during the summer months. Chicken especially seems to be
the favored choice for cookouts and picnics. Where we vaca-
tion in the Adirondacks there are a lot of wonderful spots by
lakes for eating outside, several of these places on small islands.
In spite of the fact that we have to get all provisions across the
lake in a rowboat, I still tend to take too much food, so we nearly
always have leftovers that go into the soup pot or the salad bowl
the next day. Leftover cooked chicken is perfect for this. But even
if you don't have picnic leftovers, go ahead and cook up a chicken
for a delicious summer soup. It will be a hit with grown-ups and
kids alike. Turkey is also good in spring and summer soups, as
are ham and pork in small amounts. As always, I recommend
that cooks be inventive. Use your imagination; try new things.
These soups are good teamed with any of the Simple Salads.

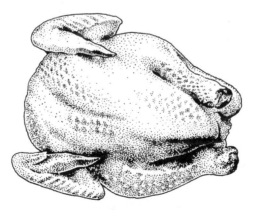

Chicken and Brown Rice, Eastern Style

It's better to start with uncooked chicken for this one, but if you want to use up some leftovers, then open a can of chicken broth to get the equivalent amount of stock.

2 chicken leg-and-thigh sections, or 3 cups cooked meat, cubed
½ cup uncooked brown rice
2 or 3 scallions, chopped
1 carrot, skinned and chopped
1 small zucchini, chopped
3 tablespoons soy sauce
1 teaspoon ground ginger
½ teaspoon chili powder
2 tablespoons rice vinegar (or other good white vinegar)
1 tablespoon minced fresh chives

Put the chicken pieces in a heavy pot with enough water to cover (at least 2 cups). Cook, covered, over medium heat for about 20 minutes, or until tender. Remove the chicken, cool, then skin it and cut the meat from the bones. Cube the meat. Skim any fat from the chicken stock and then add the rice, scallions, zucchini, soy sauce, ginger, chili powder, and vinegar. Bring to a simmer, cover, and cook until the rice is done. (Keep checking: Some brown rice takes longer than others. Instant brown rice is OK to use and takes very little time.) Stir in the chives. Serve warm.

Makes 7 or 8 cups.

Chicken, Green Beans, and Sprouts

Tender green beans from the garden and bean sprouts from the grocery are a good combination with some cooked chicken left over from a picnic or in-house dinner. Kids might balk at the sprouts, so it's best to ladle out enough soup for them before adding the offending veggies. For adventurous kids, though, leave them in.

1 garlic clove, minced
1 small onion, chopped
2 tablespoons oil, olive or vegetable
4 cups fresh green beans, ends snipped off, cut into bite-size pieces
2 cups chicken stock
2 cups cooked cubed chicken
1 cup whole milk
½ cup sour cream
1 tablespoon minced fresh herbs, such as marjoram, savory, or basil
1 cup bean sprouts

In a large, heavy pot, lightly sauté the garlic and onion in the oil. When soft, add the green beans and chicken stock. Cook uncovered for about 8 minutes, or until the beans are tender. Add the chicken, milk, sour cream, and herbs. Ladle out enough for the kids and then add the sprouts. Mix well. Season to taste with salt and pepper. Serve hot, room temperature, or cold.

Makes about 10 cups.

Green Cabbage and Chicken

When my younger son was small, he announced that cabbage was his favorite vegetable. His older brother stared at him in disbelief, but even he ate it without complaining, and over the years I have noticed that most kids like cabbage. So this recipe is for a one-pot soup that all ages should like.

While this soup has ingredients that can be found in other seasons, a fresh cabbage from the garden and new potatoes really make it a special summer soup.

2 bacon slices
1 small onion
1 garlic clove, minced
3 cups chicken stock
1 cup beef stock (or canned beef broth)
1 small green cabbage, chopped
1 apple, peeled, cored, and chopped
2 medium-size new potatoes, unpeeled, diced

In a large, heavy pot, cook the bacon until crisp and set aside, saving the drippings. In the bacon drippings, sauté the onion and garlic until lightly browned. Add the chicken and beef stocks, cabbage, apple, and potatoes; cook until the vegetables are soft. Crumble the bacon and add to the pot. Serve warm.

Makes about 10 cups.

Ground Lamb, Fennel, and Fresh Herbs

Never throw out a meat bone, especially a lamb bone. It makes a very flavorful stock and can become the base of many a good soup. If you don't have a leftover bone for this — or if your bone has no meat left on it — get a couple of shoulder chops and boil them in water to make a stock. Any meat left on the bone, whether a leg bone or shoulder-chop bone, should be ground or finely chopped, either in a food processor or by hand with a sharp knife.

1 cup cooked lamb meat, ground or finely chopped
1 tablespoon flour
3 cups lamb stock
1 fennel bulb, chopped
1 celery stalk with leaves, if any, chopped
12 or so small pearl onions
½ cup dry red wine
1 tablespoon minced fresh parsley
1 tablespoon minced fresh marjoram
1 tablespoon minced fresh mint leaves
1 tablespoon minced fresh tarragon
1 tablespoon minced chives
2 tablespoons tomato paste

In a bowl, toss the lamb with the flour to thoroughly coat. Set aside. Combine the remaining ingredients in a large pot and bring to a simmer. Cover and cook gently for about 30 minutes, or until the vegetables are soft. Spoon out some of the hot soup and add to the lamb, mixing to get a thin paste. Combine the lamb with the soup in the pot. Season to taste with salt and pepper. Serve warm.

Makes about 7 cups.

Ham, Asparagus, and Thin Noodles

This is a wonderful springtime soup, using tender stalks of fresh asparagus. All ages will like it.

> 4 tablespoons butter, or vegetable oil
> 1 cup finely chopped sweet onion
> 1 tablespoon flour
> 3 cups chicken stock, heated
> 4 cups angel-hair noodles
> 6 or 7 stalks fresh asparagus, ends broken off and stalks cut in ½-inch pieces
> 1 cup finely chopped cooked ham
> 1 cup heavy cream

Heat the butter or oil, add the onions and flour, mix well, and while stirring add the hot stock and cook until the onions are soft and the soup is slightly thickened. Add the noodles and asparagus and reduce the heat to medium. Cook until the noodles and asparagus are barely soft. Stir in the ham and cream. Season to taste with salt and pepper. Serve hot or warm.

Makes about 10 cups.

Lamb and Orzo with Cucumbers

See the Ground Lamb, Fennel, and Fresh Herbs recipe on page 61 about getting lamb and lamb stock, or use uncooked ground lamb from the market and beef stock. This recipe lends itself to both lamb and beef flavors. All ages like this. It's a good hearty supper dish for the whole family — and guests, too.

2 tablespoons oil, any kind
1 garlic clove, minced
4 cups lamb stock (or beef stock)
½ cup uncooked orzo
1 cup chopped cooked lamb (or ground lamb, fat drained off)
1 medium cucumber, peeled, seeds removed, and finely chopped.
1 tablespoon minced fresh mint leaves

Heat the oil and gently cook the garlic until it is golden. Add the lamb or beef stock and bring to a boil. Stir in the orzo, reduce the heat to medium high (enough to keep it gently boiling but not rolling), and cook until the pasta is just tender. Stir in the lamb and cucumber. Cook briefly, enough to heat lamb through and barely soften the cukes. Stir in the mint. Season to taste with salt and pepper. Serve hot or warm.

Makes about 8 cups.

Lime Chicken and Chili Peppers

This is a quick and easy recipe that can be made at the last minute. Use leftover cooked chicken and chicken stock. It's perfect for a first course or as a lunch or supper meal with a rice salad, such as Shelly's Brown Rice Salad, on the side. Delicious.

5 cups chicken stock
2 egg yolks
¼ cup lime juice
1 cup cooked chicken, finely chopped
2 tablespoons minced fresh parsley
2 green chili peppers minced
thin slices of lime for garnish

Bring the stock to a simmer. Meanwhile, in a separate bowl whisk the egg yolks. Add some hot stock to the yolks, a little at a time, whisking constantly, until it's soupy and slightly thickened. Stir in the lime juice and some more stock. Mix well. Return this mixture to the pot with the rest of the stock. Add the chicken, parsley, and chili peppers. Mix well. Season to taste with salt and pepper. Let cool. Serve cool or chilled. Garnish with a thin slice of lime.

Makes about 7 cups.

Minced Pork and Yellow Squash

This recipe works equally well with either a few shoulder chops, cooked up with the fat removed and then finely chopped, or a pound of cooked ground pork, with the fat drained off and then crumbled. If you can find a very bland sweet sausage, that will work the same as ground pork. Use your imagination.

2 tablespoons oil, olive or vegetable
1 medium-sized sweet onion
1 garlic clove, minced
1 yellow pepper, seeded and chopped
4 cups chicken stock
1 leek, white part only, thoroughly washed and thinly sliced
1 parsnip, scraped and chopped
2 teaspoons minced fresh thyme
1 teaspoon ground cumin
4 small yellow crookneck squash or yellow zucchini, to make about 4 cups
2 cups minced or finely chopped cooked pork, or cooked ground pork
1 cup sour cream

In a large pot, heat oil and sauté the onion, garlic, and yellow pepper until they are soft. Add the chicken stock, leek, parsnip, thyme, cumin, and squash. Bring to simmering and cook, covered, until vegetables are soft. Remove from heat and add the pork and sour cream. Mix well. Season to taste with salt and pepper and serve cold or warm.

Makes about 3 quarts.

Part II
SALADS

Salads have always been a featured item in my life. They were eaten for lunch and dinner, as main dishes or side dishes; they were standard on picnics, at church suppers, or barbecues. All sorts of salads: simple ones, fruits and vegetable ones, or meat and fish ones.

I especially remember the picnic salads we had in the South, probably because picnics were so special. We didn't just step out onto the lawn with salad, soup, and sandwich and eat at the picnic table the way we do at my house now. No, the picnics we had when I was a child were Outings, with a capital O. They required a lot of day-before preparations, at least one car and sometimes two, and they certainly were all-day affairs. The favorite destination was Wakulla Springs in northern Florida.

Wakulla Springs was magical for us children. Not only were there plenty of picnic tables, few other people, acres of sand with live oaks dripping Spanish moss where we could run and play, but there were the glass-bottom boats that took us out onto the crystal-clear waters of the lake-size springs. We would sit around the rim of the glass and stare down at the underwater wonders of flora and fauna, and the boat's guide would tap on the side of the boat in a certain way that called forth a pet catfish named Henry, who would be fed special treats, roll over on command, and loll under the glass staring back at us gawkers. It never occurred to us that it wasn't the same Henry every year.

Picnic food always included raw veggies, cold soup, salads, fried chicken, homemade buttered rolls (kept warm wrapped in numerous layers of linen napkins), and cookies and fruit for dessert. The fruit salads were always my favorite, with the simple green salads running a close second. This book will include those old favorites as well as new salads and new salad ideas that I hope everyone will enjoy.

Fruit Salads

M ost fruit salads are combinations of fruits, usually fresh, though there's nothing wrong with canned fruits. The fun comes with thinking up different pairings and new dressings. The following are some suggestions to work with, but remember to be inventive and add your own personal taste touches. I have tried to use only fruits and other companionable ingredients that are readily available at fruit stands and in markets. Few cooks have time to go in search of exotic items — especially in summer when outdoor pleasures beckon.

A is for Ambrosia, Apple, and Apricot:

Ambrosia Salad

This is a spin-off of that old favorite Ambrosia. It was a special dessert in the South, and I still like it, both to finish off a meal and in salad form.

2 tablespoons olive oil
1 tablespoon balsamic vinegar
1 tablespoon minced cilantro
4 cups seeded orange sections
1 cup shredded coconut
½ cup slivered almonds
spinach leaves, stems removed, to use as a bed

Combine the oil, vinegar, cilantro, oranges, coconut, and almonds. Chill. Serve on a bed of spinach leaves.

Serves 8.

Apples and Cheddar

3 cups chopped apples, red and green skins, cored but not peeled
2 heaping tablespoons mayonnaise
2 heaping tablespoons plain yogurt
1 teaspoon curry powder
1 cup chopped pecans
½ cup golden raisins
½ cup minced celery
1 small sweet onion, finely chopped
½ cup cubed sharp cheddar cheese
Bibb lettuce leaves to use as a bed

Thoroughly mix the mayonnaise, yogurt, and curry powder. Combine with the apples, pecans, raisins, celery, onion, and cheese. Serve on Bibb boats.

Serves 8 to 10.

Apricot Alley Salad

1 can (17 ounces) apricots, thinly sliced, with ¼ cup juice (discard rest)
2 tablespoons good white vinegar
1 tablespoon cumin seed
1 teaspoon turmeric
1 yellow pepper, seeded and chopped
1 cup green grapes, cut in half
1 small jar pimentos, drained and thinly sliced
torn lettuce leaves to use as a bed

Combine the apricots, vinegar, spices, pepper, grapes, and pimentos. Chill. Serve on a bed of lettuce.

Serves 8.

Beastly Sweet Fruit Salad

Kids love this, and there's enough grown-up stuff in it to appeal to the older crowd.

1 cup sliced fresh strawberries
1 banana, peeled and cubed
1 cup red seedless grapes
1 cup orange sections
2 cups fresh snow peas, barely blanched and cut in half
1 red onion, thinly slivered
½ cup chopped walnuts
1 celery stalk, finely chopped
½ cup mayonnaise thinned with ¼ cup half-and-half cream and 1 tablespoon honey
pinch of salt

Combine all the ingredients. Chill. Can be served plain or on lettuce.

Serves 8 to 10.

This recipe is also good with an oil, vinegar, Dijon mustard, and honey dressing.

C is for Cantaloupes and Cherries:

Cantaloupe Balls with Peas

Easy, easy.

1 or 2 cantaloupes, enough to make 4 cups balls
1 cup fresh peas (or frozen), lightly cooked
1 Belgian endive, washed and thinly cut crosswise into rounds
2 tablespoons olive oil
1 tablespoon white vinegar

Combine everything. That's it.

Serves 8 to 10.

Cherries, Cukes, and Cherry Tomatoes

4 cups (or more) mixed salad greens
3 tablespoons olive oil
1 tablespoon lemon juice
2 cups stemmed and pitted dark red cherries
1 cucumber, peeled, seeded, and chopped
2 cups small cherry tomatoes
¼ cup crumbled feta cheese

Toss the greens with the oil, lemon juice, and salt and pepper to taste. Add the cherries, cukes, tomatoes, and cheese, and lightly mix. Serve cold.

Serves 8.

Frozen Fruit Salad

This is an old-fashioned favorite in the South. In days gone by, drug-stores even sold it at the counter, along with the Cokes, potato chips, and ice cream. Most cooks had their own special recipe for this, and all the ones I ever ate were delicious. I think most recipes used canned fruits, but certainly fresh fruits, lightly poached in syrup water, can be used. Following is a recipe given to me a long time ago, and I can't resist not including it. Cholesterol watchers, beware!

    1 1-pound can (16 ounces) mixed fruit, drained and fruit chopped
    1 small can pears, drained and fruit chopped
    1 small can crushed pineapple, drained
    2 small bananas, cut into small chunks
    ½ cup mayonnaise
    1 tablespoon lemon juice
    1 tablespoon sugar
    ½ pint heavy cream, whipped
    pinch of salt
    lettuce for bed

Combine all the ingredients except the lettuce. Pour into ice trays or a plastic container the size of an ice-cream carton. Freeze. Serve on lettuce and eat at once. Good to use as a first course.

Serves 12 or more.

Grapes Galore

Everyone will enjoy the nice blend of colors of this recipe.

½ cup cottage cheese
1 tablespoon minced basil
1 tablespoon lemon juice
2 cups seedless green grapes
2 cups seedless red grapes
½ cup slivered almonds
radicchio, broken up, and fresh spinach leaves, stemmed, for a bed

In a blender or food processor, puree the cottage cheese. Add the basil and lemon juice (and salt to taste) if desired. Combine this mixture with the grapes and almonds, and serve on radicchio and spinach leaves.

Serves 8.

Kiwi Green

3 tablespoons olive oil
1 tablespoon lime juice
1 tablespoon minced thyme
4 ripe kiwis, peeled and chopped
1 ripe avocado, peeled and sliced
1 green pepper, seeded and thinly sliced
½ sweet onion, thinly sliced
spinach leaves for a bed

Combine oil, lime juice, and thyme; add salt and pepper to taste. Mix with the kiwis, avocado, pepper, and onion. Serve on a bed of spinach.

Serves 6 to 8.

P is for Pears and Pineapple:

Pears, Apples, and Pecans on Endive Spears

> 2 ripe soft and sweet pears (any variety), peeled, cored, and sliced
> 1 green apple (such as a Granny Smith), cored and sliced (do not peel)
> 1 cup seedless red grapes, cut in half
> ½ cup pecans, chopped
> endive spears as a bed
> 3 tablespoons oil
> 1 tablespoon vinegar
> pinch of salt
> crumbled blue cheese

Arrange the fruits and pecans on endive spears. Mix the oil, vinegar, and salt and drizzle over all. Sprinkle on the blue cheese.

Serves 6 to 8.

Pineapple, Cukes, and Ham

> 3 tablespoons olive oil
> 1 tablespoon lemon juice, mixed
> 1 fresh pineapple, rind removed, cored, and fruit cut into chunks
> 2 cucumbers, peeled, seeded, and chopped
> 1 sweet onion, such as Vidalia, chopped
> ½ cup chopped walnuts
> ¼ cup minced fresh mint leaves
> 1 cup diced cooked ham
> 1 tablespoon sweet pickle relish
> lettuce leaves for a bed

Mix the oil and lemon juice. Combine all the ingredients except the lettuce. Serve on a bed of lettuce leaves.

Serves 10 to 12.

White Salads — Rice, Potato, & Pasta

Most white salads can be made ahead of time and refrigerated until ready to use. I do include one potato salad that should be served warm, and in fact it wouldn't hurt any of these salads to be served at room temperature. The coldness of the dish depends on the cook's time: If it's easier to prepare the salad ahead of time, do it. Remember, the comfort of the cook is right behind the tastiness of the meal. Use these recipes as guides and add whatever you have on hand that you think would be an interesting addition.

RICE SALADS

Fanciful Rice Salad with Pine Nuts and Parmesan

    3 cups cooked rice
    1 cup cooked green beans, cut up
    1 garlic clove, minced
    ¼ cup pine nuts, lightly toasted
    ¼ cup freshly grated Parmesan cheese

Dressing:
    4 tablespoons olive oil
    1 tablespoon white vinegar
    3 tablespoons minced basil

Combine all the salad ingredients. Toss with the dressing. Serve plain or on a bed of shredded lettuce.

Serves 8 to 10.

Grab-bag Rice and Peas Salad

    3 cups cooked rice
    1 cup green peas, lightly cooked
    ½ of a small sweet onion, slivered
    ¼ cup black olives, chopped

Dressing:
    ¼ cup mayonnaise
    2 tablespoons plain yogurt
    1 tablespoon minced mint

Combine all the salad ingredients. Toss with the dressing.

Serves 8.

Green Rice

1 cup raw rice
2 cups chicken stock
1 packed cup chopped fresh spinach, or ½ cup frozen chopped
    spinach, thawed
½ cup chopped parsley
1 garlic clove, minced
1 medium-sized sweet onion, chopped
2 tablespoons oil, olive or vegetable, plus 1 teaspoon water

Combine the rice and chicken stock in a saucepan and bring to a simmer, stirring to keep it from settling on the bottom. Cover; cook over low heat for about 20 minutes, or until the rice is done. In a separate pan, combine the remaining ingredients and cook briefly over very low heat, until the spinach is tender. Add to the rice and mix well. Cool. Season with salt to taste.

Serves 6 to 8.

Red Rice

2 cups raw rice
1 medium can chopped peeled tomatoes, with juice
1 ½ cups chicken stock
2 hard-boiled eggs, chopped
1 red onion, chopped

Dressing:
2 tablespoons oil
1 tablespoon lemon juice

Cook the rice in the tomatoes and stock mixture, over low heat and covered, until tender. Combine with remaining ingredients. Cool. Season to taste with salt and pepper.

Serves 8.

Shelly's Brown Rice Salad

Shelly is the wife of my sons' best friend — a great girl and a good cook. She and her family live in California, where the traditional cuisine is light and refreshing, and she has learned to cook accordingly. This delicious salad of hers fits the bill. Kids and adults all like it. It's a wonderful summer salad to accompany any kind of meat. Vegetarians will like it as a main dish.

    1 cup raw brown rice
    1 cucumber, peeled and diced
    1 tomato, diced
    ¼ cup slivered almonds
    2 tablespoons olive oil
    juice of 2 lemons, about 1/4 cup

Cook the rice according to package directions. Drain. Mix with remaining ingredients. Serve cold, either plain or on a bed of lettuce.

Serves 6 to 8.

Wild Rice with Figs and Nuts

Wild rice isn't really rice at all — it's grass — but I've included it here anyway.

    ½ cup cut-up dried figs
    ½ cup chicken stock
    3 tablespoons olive oil
    1 tablespoon balsamic vinegar
    1 tablespoon minced sage
    2 cups cooked wild rice
    ¼ cup chopped pecans

Combine the figs and chicken stock in a saucepan, bring to a simmer, cover, and cook for 4 or 5 minutes. Remove from the heat and let stand until the figs have plumped. Combine the oil, vinegar, and sage. Mix with the cooked wild rice, the figs, the remains of the stock, and the pecans. Season to taste with salt and pepper. Serve at room temperature or cold.

Serves 6.

Yellow Rice with Summer Squash and Pine Nuts

    1 cup raw rice
    2 cups chicken stock
    1 teaspoon turmeric
    1 teaspoon curry powder
    2 medium-sized yellow summer squash, coarsely chopped
    3 tablespoons oil, vegetable or olive
    ¼ cup pine nuts
    ½ cup golden raisins

Simmer the rice in the chicken stock with the turmeric and curry powder for about 20 minutes, or until tender. In a separate pan, sauté the squash in the oil until tender. Combine the rice and squash. Add the pine nuts and raisins. Chill.

Serves 8.

POTATO SALADS

Most people have a favorite way of making potato salad. Following are three recipes my family likes. All of them are easy, and kids like them as well as adults.

Leek and Potato Salad

    1 leek, thoroughly washed, tippy-top green part removed, rest
        chopped with white part
    3 tablespoons oil plus 1 tablespoon water
    6 medium-sized new potatoes, unpeeled, cooked (though still
        firm), and coarsely chopped
    1 tablespoon sesame seeds, lightly toasted in oven
    1 tablespoon white vinegar
    dash of paprika

Simmer the leek in the oil and water mix until tender. Cool. Mix with the remaining ingredients. Season to taste with salt and pepper.

Serves 8.

Mimi's Warm Potato Salad

Mimi, the grandmother of my best friend, was a wonderful cook. She never measured anything, just adding and tasting as she went. This is the way I recall her potato salad.

    6 large potatoes, cooked, peeled, and sliced.
    3 bacon slices
    1 onion, chopped
    3 tablespoons white vinegar
    1 tablespoon minced dillweed

Cook the bacon until crisp; lift out slices (reserving the drippings) and crumble. In the bacon fat, sauté the onion until soft. Combine all the ingredients in a bowl. Serve warm or at room temperature.

Serves 10 to 12.

Mustard Potato Salad with Sorrel

Sorrel has a wonderful tart flavor that adds zip to any dish. Sorrel soup is excellent, and a little sorrel added to summer squash or fresh green beans is a good touch for these vegetables. It also works wonderfully in this salad, which uses thin-skinned new potatoes.

    10 to 12 small new potatoes, cooked
    1 cup sorrel leaves, thoroughly washed and chopped
    1 tablespoon prepared mustard, such as Dijon
    1 tablespoon lemon juice
    2 tablespoons olive oil
    1 green apple, cored and diced
    ¼ cup chopped walnuts
    ¼ cup finely chopped prosciutto (or other Italian ham)

Cook the potatoes, skins on, and coarsely cube when cooled. Combine the sorrel, mustard, lemon juice, and oil. Stir in the apple, walnuts, and prosciutto. Toss all these ingredients with the potatoes.

Serves 6 to 8.

This salad is good with anything.

PASTA SALADS

About 20 years ago I served a pasta salad, and everyone thought I had gone over the edge or was too lazy to turn on the oven. Now these salads abound around the world — anywhere pasta is sold, there's a pasta-salad recipe lurking nearby. Here are some ideas.

Antipasto Pasta Salad

Antipasti are usually meats, cheeses, and marinated vegetables that precede the first course and the pasta (or, for controlled eaters, main) course of the meal. Putting the antipasti and pasta together simplifies serving, especially if outdoor dining is planned.

    ½ cup cooked white tuna chunks (canned is fine here)
    3 or 4 anchovies, chopped (but only if you're serving adults; most
        kids don't like these)
    ¼ cup diced ham
    ½ cup cubed mozzarella
    ½ red pepper, seeded and diced
    1 large ripe tomato, chopped
    1 hard-boiled egg, chopped
    1 small cucumber, peeled and chopped
    3 or 4 mushrooms, chopped
    4 cups cooked (al dente) pasta, such as ziti or twists

Dressing:
    ¼ cup olive oil
    2 tablespoons good vinegar
    1 tablespoon minced herbs (such as basil, marjoram, oregano, or
        parsley)

Combine all the ingredients. Toss with the dressing. Serve cold or at room temperature.

Serves 8 to 10.

Corn and Chinese Cabbage with Pasta and Lentils

    4 cups cooked tubular pasta, such as ziti or rigatoni
    2 cups cooked fresh corn kernels
    2 packed cups of shredded Chinese cabbage, blanched
    1 red onion, chopped
    1 cup green grapes
    1 cup cooked lentils
    ¼ cup oil, olive or vegetable
    2 tablespoons balsamic vinegar
    ¼ cup crumbled feta cheese

Combine all the ingredients. Season to taste with salt and pepper.
Serve cold.

Serves 12.

Fettuccini Red and Green

While green spinach fettuccini is usually served warm, this combination makes a good cold salad. The light and dark green with the red is quite colorful.

    4 cups cooked spinach fettuccini, broken into 1-inch pieces before
        cooking
    1 cup red-stemmed Swiss chard (both green tops and red stems),
        chopped and blanched
    1 cup baby tomatoes, either red cherry or red grape
    1 clove garlic, minced
    1 red pepper, seeded and slivered

Dressing:
    2 tablespoons olive oil
    1 tablespoon white vinegar

Combine all the salad ingredients. Toss with the dressing. Season to taste with salt and pepper. Serve cold.

Serves 8.

Macaroni Creole Salad

This is an old South Georgia recipe given to me many years ago. It travels well and is great for picnics. Make this in advance and refrigerate.

4 cups cooked (al dente) macaroni
2 cups diced ripe tomatoes
1 cup shredded cheddar cheese
1 cup finely chopped celery
1 garlic clove, minced
½ cup chopped pitted green olives
1 cup mayonnaise mixed with ½ teaspoon cayenne pepper

Combine all the ingredients. Chill. Good when served on a bed of lettuce.

Serves 8 to 10.

Twists and Cukes

3 cups cooked (al dente) pasta twists
1 medium cucumber, peeled, seeded, and cut in thin short julienne strips
3 or 4 chopped canned artichoke hearts
3 tablespoons grated Parmesan cheese
¼ cup mayonnaise
¼ cup plain yogurt

Mix the mayo and yogurt; combine with everything else. Season to taste with salt and pepper.

Serves 8.

Ziti with Mushrooms, Ginger, and Tuna

The tangy sweet crystallized ginger mixed with the mushrooms and tuna give this a really nice flavor. All ages should like it. (By sautéing the mushrooms quickly in hot oil, the brown juices stay in the mushrooms instead of causing them to float in liquid. This makes a better color when combined with the pasta.)

2 tablespoons oil, olive or vegetable
1 cup cut-up tasty mushrooms, such as shiitake or porcini
3 cups cooked (al dente) ziti
3 tablespoons finely chopped crystallized ginger
1 cup flaked white tuna (canned tuna is OK)
1 teaspoon fresh lemon juice
1 teaspoon dry white wine

Heat the oil and quickly sauté the mushrooms until barely tender and browned. Remove from heat. Combine the mushrooms and oil with the cooked ziti, the ginger, and the tuna. Sprinkle on the lemon juice and wine and gently toss. Season to taste with salt and pepper. Serve at room temperature or cold.

Serves 8.

Main Dish Salads

Main-dish salads are just what the name implies. Some are made with chicken, beef, or other meats; some with seafood or fish; some are for vegetarians. My son and his family, who live in Washington D.C., where the summers are long, hot, and steamy, eat a lot of main-dish salads. They have a beautiful small tree-shaded patio behind the house, and the kids especially enjoy eating outside. Salads, served with a crusty baguette and a bowl of fresh fruit in the center of the table, are mainstays most nights.

The great thing about these salads is making them ahead of time — even early morning, before the heat of the day gets intense and makes the kitchen take second place to a pool or shady garden or air-conditioned office — then refrigerating them until ready to eat. Those lazy, hazy days of summer are perfect settings for the following dishes.

Salads with chicken, beef, and other meats are listed first, followed by fish and seafood, and then vegetarian salads. Good breads — whether dense, crusty loaves or muffins or delicate dinner rolls — are good accompaniments. Fruit and sorbets go well with this menu. And don't forget those Spring and Summer Soups that always make good starters!

SALADS WITH CHICKEN, BEEF AND OTHER MEATS

Abbie's Chicken Salad with Grapes

My daughter-in-law Abbie uses chicken breasts and green grapes for this salad, but I think dark meat and red grapes would also be good, though different. She serves this with a tossed green salad and a warm baguette. A delicious summer meal — and the three little ones usually eat at least two helpings of everything.

> 3 boned chicken breasts, split (6 halves), cooked and cut into cubes
> 2 cups green grapes
> ¼ cup minced celery
> ½ cup, more or less, mayonnaise (or a mayonnaise and plain yogurt combination)

Combine all the ingredients. Season to taste with salt and pepper, and chill.

Serves 8.

Chicken-'n-Rice with Black Beans and Broccoli

> 4 cups cubed cooked chicken breasts (about 5 halves)
> 2 cups cooked white rice
> 3 cups broccoli florets and some cut-up stems
> 1 tablespoon oil plus 2 tablespoons water and 1 tablespoon lemon juice
> 1 ½ cups cooked black beans, rinsed (canned ones are fine)
> additional 3 tablespoons oil and 2 tablespoons vinegar
> 3 cups shredded lettuce for a bed

In a large bowl, combine the chicken and rice and set aside. Cook the broccoli in oil, water, and lemon juice mix until barely soft. Mix with the chicken and rice and add the black beans. Add additional oil and vinegar. Season to taste with salt and pepper. Chill. Serve on a bed of shredded lettuce.

Serves 8 to 10.

Curried Lamb with Garden Peas Salad

Fresh peas make any dish taste good. Combined with lamb and a little curry powder, the dish becomes extra special. (In a pinch, a combination of chili powder, cayenne, and ginger is a good substitute for curry powder.) This is good served with a little chutney.

    3 cups cooked cubed lamb
    2 cups fresh peas, barely cooked
    1 clove garlic, minced
    1 tablespoon shredded coconut

Dressing:
    3 tablespoons olive oil
    2 tablespoons lemon juice
    1 tablespoon curry powder

Combine the oil, lemon juice, and curry powder. Toss with the remaining ingredients. Season to taste with salt and pepper.

Serves 4 to 6.

Five Cs Salad

    2 cups shredded green cabbage
    2 celery stalks, finely chopped
    3 or 4 carrots, shredded
    3 tablespoons minced chives
    2 cups chopped cooked chicken
    1 medium-sized Vidalia onion, chopped
    3 tablespoons minced mint leaves

Dressing:
    ¼ cup oil, walnut or olive
    2 tablespoons white vinegar
    2 tablespoons lime juice
    1 teaspoon sugar

Mix the dressing ingredients. Combine with everything else. Season to taste with salt and pepper.

Serves 8.

Ground Lamb and Black Beans

White beans are more traditional with lamb, but this is a nice change.

    1 pound ground lamb, cooked and drained
    2 cups black beans, rinsed
    1 large ripe tomato, chopped
    1 teaspoon cinnamon

Dressing:
    4 tablespoons oil, olive or vegetable
    1 tablespoon lemon juice
    1 tablespoon dry white wine

Mix the dressing ingredients. Combine with everything else. Season to taste with salt and pepper.

Serves 6 to 8.

This salad is pleasing to look at when served on shredded lettuce.

Lamb and White Bean Salad

Here's the traditional combination, using some leftover lamb.

    1 cup cooked cubed lamb
    1 cup cooked white beans
    1 cup lightly steamed zucchini cubes
    1 ripe tomato, chopped
    Romaine leaves to use as boats

Dressing:
    2 tablespoons olive oil
    2 heaping tablespoons plain yogurt
    1 teaspoon minced cilantro leaves

Mix the dressing ingredients. Combine with the lamb, beans, zucchini, and tomato. Season to taste with salt and pepper. Serve on Romaine leaves.

Serves 6.

Marinated Steak and Chard Salad

This is good for a Sunday lunch buffet — other times, too. I've served it with Cauliflower Plus soup, rice, sliced garden tomatoes, and hard rolls.

1 large steak, sirloin or other tender cut, broiled to medium rare
1 bunch red or green Swiss chard, tender stems and green tops, cut up and steamed
3 tablespoons olive oil
1 tablespoon balsamic vinegar

Slice the steak into strips and then cut into 1-inch pieces for manageable eating. Toss with the remaining ingredients. Season to taste with salt and pepper

Serves 4 to 6.

Meatloaf and Potato Salad

When making a meat loaf, make an extra-large one so there will be some left over for this combination.

2 cups cubed cooked meat loaf
6 or so small new potatoes (with skin), lightly cooked and quartered
2 ripe tomatoes, chopped
1 cucumber, peeled and chopped
2 tablespoons fresh herbs, such as basil, marjoram, or thyme
shredded lettuce

Dressing:
½ cup mayonnaise
2 tablespoons oil
2 tablespoons tomato juice

Mix the dressing ingredients. Combine with the remaining ingredients. Serve with shredded lettuce as a base.

Serves 6 or 7.

Minced Ham Salad

This is a good way to use some leftover cooked ham.

    2 cups minced ham
    1 cucumber, peeled and finely chopped
    1 green apple, cored and finely chopped
    1 tablespoon minced tarragon
    1 cup toasted croutons
    lettuce as a bed

Dressing:
    2 tablespoons oil
    2 tablespoons plain yogurt
    2 tablespoons lemon juice

Mix the dressing ingredients. Toss with everything else. Serve on a bed of lettuce — before the croutons get soggy.

Serves 6.

Pineapple Ham

If a fresh pineapple can't be found, use drained canned pineapple chunks.

    ½ cup mayonnaise
    1 tablespoon prepared mustard
    2 cups pineapple cubes
    2 cups cubed cooked ham
    1 green pepper, slivered
    1 celery stalk, finely chopped
    head of Bibb lettuce

Mix the mayonnaise and mustard. Combine with the rest of the ingredients. Serve in Bibb boats.

Serves 6 to 8.

Stir-fried Beef and Peppers

If you want a fun meal that stirs up the taste buds, try this with Curried Cucumber and Grape Soup, with some rice on the side. Use a wok or a heavy frying pan for this one.

  1 pound tender beef, cut into thin strips
  1 red pepper, seeded and slivered
  1 green pepper, seeded and slivered.
  1 yellow pepper, seeded and slivered
  1 garlic clove, minced
  ¼ cup oil, olive or vegetable
  1 Belgian endive, cut into thin rounds
  2 tablespoons lemon juice
  1 tablespoon Worcestershire sauce
  lettuce for a bed

Heat the oil and quickly sauté the meat and peppers, turning constantly to evenly brown. Add the endive and cook briefly to barely wilt it. Remove from the heat. Mix the lemon juice and Worcestershire and add to the beef. Season to taste with salt and pepper. Cool to room temperature. Serve on a bed of lettuce.

Serves 6.

Turkey with Chickpeas

A good mix.

  ¼ cup olive oil
  2 tablespoons lemon juice
  2 cups cubed cooked turkey
  1 can (16 ounces) chickpeas, drained
  1 ripe tomato, chopped
  ½ cup chopped fresh parsley

Mix the oil and lemon juice. Combine with all the other ingredients. Season to taste with salt and pepper. Serve cold.

Serves 6.

Watercress and Chicken

A wild watercress bed grows not too far from me in southern Vermont. These freshly cut leaves are unbelievably tender with a distinctive bite to the taste, but domesticated cress beds also produce delicious leaves — one of the rewards of summer.

4 cups cubed cooked chicken
2 cups watercress leaves
1 celery stalk, minced
1 apple, cored and finely chopped
2 hard-boiled eggs, chopped

Dressing:
¼ cup olive oil
2 tablespoons white vinegar
1 teaspoon prepared mustard

Mix the dressing ingredients. Combine with everything else. Season to taste with salt and pepper.

Serves 6 to 8.

Wilted Greens with Spicy Pork

This is a good way to use some leftover cooked pork, a roasted loin or baked chops.

¼ cup oil, olive or vegetable
2 tablespoons lime juice
1 tablespoon chili powder
1 tablespoon ground ginger
¼ teaspoon cayenne pepper
4 cups spinach leaves
2 cups chard leaves
1 cup turnip greens (leaves only)
3 cups cooked cubed pork
1 green pepper, seeded and finely chopped
1 egg, hard-boiled and chopped

Combine oil, lime juice, and spices and heat in a large pan. Wet the spinach, chard leaves, and turnip greens with water and add them to the pan. Cook briefly until the greens have wilted. Remove from the heat and stir in the pork, green pepper, and hard-boiled eggs. Season to taste with salt and pepper.

Serves 6 to 8.

SALADS WITH FISH AND SEAFOOD

Most kids like tuna fish, especially in sandwiches. Salmon loaf is another good bet when testing young taste buds. Then there's plain old-fashioned fish like trout, bass, catfish, and the like, and most young will eat these (there's always an exception somewhere). So fish and seafood salads will probably be eaten by all ages — certainly try them.

Apple Tuna Salad

    3 tablespoons mayonnaise
    1 tablespoon plain yogurt
    1 teaspoon sweet relish
    2 cups flaked cooked tuna (white, if canned)
    1 celery stalk, finely chopped
    ½ small sweet onion, finely chopped
    1 apple, cored and chopped
    lettuce for a bed

Mix the mayo, yogurt, and relish. Combine with the remaining ingredients. Serve on lettuce.

Serves 6.

Cajun Tuna and Rice

This is based on the old favorite in France of tuna and rice salad. As the French influence in the Cajun regions of Louisiana is still strong, I have put the two nationalities together.

2 cups flaked cooked tuna
2 cups cooked rice
¼ cup minced cilantro leaves
1 garlic clove, minced
1 yellow pepper, seeded and chopped

Dressing:
¼ cup mayonnaise
2 tablespoons cider vinegar
½ teaspoon ground cumin
¼ teaspoon cayenne pepper

Mix the dressing ingredients. Combine with the remaining ingredients.
Serves 6.

Crab Salad with Saucy Carrots

¼ cup mayonnaise
2 tablespoons lemon juice
1 tablespoon ground ginger
1 cup shredded carrots
½ cup golden raisins
1 cup ready-to-eat lump crabmeat, fresh or frozen
2 large tomatoes, sliced into 6 rounds
shredded lettuce as a garnish

Mix the mayo, lemon juice, and ginger. Stir in the carrots and raisins. Salt to taste. Stir in the crab. Serve on slices of tomatoes with a little shredded lettuce around the edges.

Serves 6.

Scallops with Grilled Peaches

Use summer-sweet fresh peaches for this.

    3 tablespoons oil, olive or vegetable
    4 large ripe peaches, peeled, pitted, and cut into slices
    1 pound sea scallops, cut in half
    1 celery stalk, minced
    3 tablespoons dry white wine
    shredded lettuce as a bed

Heat the oil and add the peach slices; sauté until lightly brown but still firm. Add the scallops and cook briefly, until they become slightly firm. Remove from the heat and add the celery and wine. Season to taste with salt and pepper. Serve on a bed of shredded lettuce.

Serves 6 to 8.

Shrimp with Spinach and Bean Sprouts

Before adding the bean sprouts, put enough salad for the kids in a separate bowl. Most of them don't appreciate the sprouts' crispy virtues.

    3 tablespoons olive oil
    1 tablespoon tarragon vinegar
    1 tablespoon minced basil
    1 pound cooked shrimp, heads and tails removed and deveined
        (if large, cut in half)
    3 cups fresh spinach leaves
    1 cup bean sprouts
    ½ cup slivered almonds

Combine the oil, vinegar, and basil. Mix with the remaining ingredients. Chill.

Serves 6 to 8.

Tropical Lobster Salad

If a mango isn't available in your market, use a peach.

    4 tablespoons oil
    2 tablespoons plain yogurt
    1 teaspoon minced tarragon
    ½ teaspoon dry mustard
    ½ teaspoon cumin seed
    3 cups cut-up lobster meat
    1 cup pineapple chunks
    1 mango, peeled, pitted, and chopped
    ¼ cup shredded coconut
    1 cup fresh green peas, blanched
    1 celery stalk, minced
    1 cup tiny cherry tomatoes

Combine the oil, yogurt, tarragon, mustard, and cumin seed. Mix with the remaining ingredients in a large bowl. Serve cold.

Serves 8 to 10.

Vegetarian Salads

The bountiful produce of summer is a vegetarian's delight. There are so many choices from markets and the garden, and the combinations are endless. The young I know usually eat vegetables without any fuss, though there has been an exception or two to this over the years. My sons had a friend who frequently came to visit when they were all quite small, and he would eat no vegetables or fruits at all (he only ate cereal, whole wheat bread, and Vienna sausages.) But he grew up to be healthy and normal — and I believe now eats well-rounded meals just like the rest of them. So don't worry if you get someone who doesn't like vegetables. Time changes most things for the better.

Bread and Cucumber Panzanella

Panzanellas are traditional Italian bread salads. Each cook adds ingredients to suit personal taste. Just remember to use firm bread, such as sour dough or day-old white or wheat cut in thick slices. Fresh ripe vegetables from the garden or market do the rest.

⅓ cup olive oil
3 tablespoons wine vinegar
2 tablespoons chopped basil
1 garlic clove, minced
2 cups cubed firm bread, toasted
5 or 6 ripe Italian plum tomatoes
1 cucumber, peeled and coarsely chopped
1 small sweet onion, chopped
1 yellow pepper, seeded and slivered

Mix the oil, vinegar, basil, and garlic. Combine with the remaining ingredients. Season to taste with salt and pepper.

Serves 8.

Broccoli Niçoise Panzanella

Omit capers and anchovies if fussy kids are eating — or halve the amounts.

⅓ cup olive oil
3 tablespoons lemon juice
3 tablespoons chopped basil
1 teaspoon capers
2 tablespoons minced anchovies
3 cups cubed firm bread, toasted
2 cups broccoli florets, cut up
1 small sweet onion, chopped
1 cup drained black olives
2 hard-boiled eggs, chopped
1 small cucumber, peeled and chopped
1 garlic clove, minced

Combine the oil, lemon juice, basil, capers, and anchovies. Mix with the remaining ingredients. Season with salt to taste.

Serves 8.

Cabbage and Chickpeas Panzanella

⅓ cup olive oil
3 tablespoons vinegar
1 tablespoon chopped chives
2 cups cubed firm bread, toasted
1 cup finely shredded green cabbage
1 cup drained chickpeas
1 clove garlic, minced
½ cucumber, peeled and chopped
2 ripe tomatoes, chopped
¼ cup crumbled Feta cheese

Combine the oil, vinegar, and chives. Mix with the remaining ingredients. Season to taste with salt and pepper.

Serves 6 to 8.

Cabbage and Peas with Brown Rice

¼ cup oil
3 tablespoons vinegar
1 tablespoon cumin seed
1 teaspoon ground ginger
1 small fresh green cabbage, finely slivered
1 cup green peas, barely cooked
¼ cup scallions, chopped
1 carrot, grated
2 cups cooked brown rice

Combine the oil, vinegar, cumin seed, and ginger. Mix with the remaining ingredients. Season to taste with salt and pepper.

Serves 8.

Corny Pepper-stuffed Toms

4 large ripe tomatoes, halved, meat scooped out and chopped
2 cups cooked orzo
1 cup cooked corn kernels
1 red pepper, seeded and chopped
¼ cup minced cilantro
¼ cup plain yogurt
¼ cup olive oil
2 tablespoons lime juice
lettuce as a bed

Combine the tomato meat, orzo, corn, pepper, cilantro, yogurt, oil, and lime juice. Season to taste with salt and pepper. Fill the 8 tomato-halves with the mixture. Serve on a bed of lettuce.

Serves 8.

Curried Shells and Corn

    3 cups cooked (al dente) pasta shells
    1 cup cooked corn kernels
    1 Vidalia onion, chopped
    1 cup cherry tomatoes
    ½ cup pine nuts, lightly toasted
    2 tablespoons minced marjoram

Dressing:
    ⅓ cup oil
    3 tablespoons vinegar
    2 tablespoons sweet sherry
    2 tablespoons curry powder

Combine the dressing ingredients. Mix with everything else. Season to taste with salt and pepper.

Serves 6.

Eggplant and Onion Salad

    ⅓ cup oil, olive or vegetable
    1 small eggplant, chopped
    1 sweet onion, chopped
    1 ripe tomato, chopped
    1 cup cooked corn kernels
    ½ cup shredded cheddar cheese
    3 tablespoons red wine vinegar
    1 tablespoon minced chives
    1 garlic clove, minced
    lettuce as a bed

Heat the oil and cook the eggplant, stirring, until barely soft. Remove from the heat and cool. Add the onion, tomato, corn, and cheese. In a separate small bowl, mix the vinegar, chives, garlic, and salt and pepper to taste. Combine with the eggplant mixture. Chill. Serve on torn lettuce pieces.

Serves 6 to 8.

Leila's Tabbouleh

My sister-in-law Leila lived in the Middle East for many years when her husband was in the U.S. Foreign Service. She diligently studied the geography, cultural monuments, native people, customs, clothes, and food wherever they lived or traveled. She brought back wonderful recipes, including this one, which is a vegetarian's summer delight.

1 cup uncooked wheat bulgur
2 cups boiling water
1 clove garlic, minced
¼ teaspoon ground allspice
¼ cup finely chopped mint leaves
1 scallion, finely chopped
1 cup finely chopped parsley
1 large ripe tomato, diced
¼ cup lemon juice
⅓ cup olive oil
½ teaspoon salt (or more to taste)
Romaine lettuce

Pour the boiling water over the bulgur and let it stand for 1 to 2 hours, until fluffy. Add the remaining ingredients and toss gently. Chill. Serve on Romaine lettuce leaves as boats.

Serves 6 to 8.

Main Street Coleslaw

½ cup mayonnaise (or more)
¼ cup white vinegar
1 teaspoon sugar
small green cabbage, finely shredded
1 apple, cored and chopped
1 cup green peas, blanched
½ cup drained chickpeas
1 garlic clove, minced
1 carrot, shredded
¼ cup golden raisins
¼ cup bottled green olives, chopped

Combine the mayo, vinegar, and sugar. Mix with the remaining ingredients. Add salt and pepper to taste. Chill.

Serves 8.

Mimosa Salad

2 cups cut green beans, blanched
1 cup red radishes, sliced
1 cup orange sections (canned Mandarin are OK)
½ cup slivered almonds, lightly toasted
1 avocado, peeled, pitted, and cut in thin strips

Dressing:
4 tablespoons olive oil
2 tablespoons lemon juice
1 teaspoon minced oregano
pinch of salt

Combine the dressing ingredients. Toss with the beans, radishes, oranges, and almonds. Top the salad with avocado slices. Serve chilled.

Serves 8

Scandinavian Veggie Salad

This is easy to double or triple for a big buffet. Serve chilled.

½ cup sour cream
2 tablespoons wine vinegar
2 tablespoons minced dillweed
2 cups of blanched green peas
2 cups blanched diced carrots
1 cup diced cooked beets
1 celery stalk, minced
1 garlic clove, minced

Combine the sour cream, vinegar, and dill. Mix with the remaining ingredients. Season to taste with salt.

Serves 8.

Tri-color Salad

1 red onion, chopped
1 red pepper, seeded and chopped
2 cups cooked white beans (such as Great Northern)
1 stalk celery, finely chopped
1 green pepper, seeded and chopped
1 cup cooked green beans, chopped
¼ cup chopped basil

Dressing:
¼ cup olive oil
3 tablespoons vinegar
2 tablespoons white wine

Mix the dressing ingredients. Toss with everything else. Season to taste with salt and pepper. Chill.

Serves 6 to 8.

Two-Bean Couscous in Portobello Cups

¼ cup olive oil
6 portobello mushroom caps, stems removed

Filling:
2 cups cooked couscous
1 cup cooked white beans, such as cannellini
1 cup cooked black beans
2 ripe tomatoes, chopped
1 small cucumber, peeled and chopped
2 firm ripe peaches, peeled, pitted, and chopped
½ cup black olives, chopped
¼ cup grated Parmesan cheese
4 tablespoons white vinegar
4 tablespoons cream sherry
shredded lettuce as a bed

Heat the oil in a large, flat skillet. Place the mushrooms in oil with the inside of the caps facing down. Cook them quickly in the hot oil to barely soften. Remove and cool. Mix the remaining ingredients with any oil left in the pan, adding salt and pepper to taste. Fill the mushroom caps. Serve with some shredded lettuce under and around the caps.

Serves 8.

Simple Salads

Beet and Fennel Salad

Combine cooked chopped beets with thin slices of fennel bulb, Belgian endive cut across in thin circles, and cored chopped green apple. Add oil and vinegar. Salt to taste.

Blair's Green Salad with Oranges and Blue Cheese

This is a favorite of my daughter-in-law Blair. She uses a variety of greens (mesclun mix, torn lettuces, or spinach), combined with drained canned Mandarin oranges and crumbled blue cheese. Serve with oil-and-vinegar dressing.

Chopped Tomatoes and Chives

Peel and chop ripe tomatoes (at least one per person). Add some minced chives. Mix sour cream with some mayonnaise and spoon on top of individual servings.

Greens with Apples and Feta

Combination of lettuces, spinach leaves, and watercress with cored and chopped firm apples and crumbled feta cheese. Add oil-and-vinegar dressing.

Onions, Cucumbers, and Pears with Blue Cheese

Combine a chopped sweet onion and a peeled chopped cucumber with cored, chopped ripe firm pears and crumbled blue cheese. Add oil-and-vinegar dressing.

Peaches with Radicchio

Combine firm ripe peaches (peeled, pitted, and sliced thin) with chopped escarole and chopped walnuts. Mix sour cream and yogurt, add to peaches, season to taste, and serve on radicchio.

Simple Salad of Greens and Toms

Lettuce leaves, spinach leaves, fresh green herbs, and ripe tomatoes. Serve with oil-and-vinegar dressing. For variety, add chopped peeled cucumber or chopped sweet onion.

Spinach, Corn, and Red Onion Salad

Fresh spinach leaves (no stems), cooked corn kernels, and chopped red onion. Good with oil, lemon juice, herbs, and crumbled feta cheese.

Squash, Onion, and Peas

Summer squash (either yellow crookneck or zucchini), blanched and cubed. Add chopped sweet onion and blanched green peas. Any dressing will work.

Tomato and Chili Peppers

Combine chopped tomatoes with chives, cooked corn kernels, and minced hot peppers. Add oil, lemon juice, salt, and pepper. Serve on lettuce boats. (The corn may be omitted.)

Watercress and Rice

Add lots of chopped watercress to cooked rice. Add pine nuts; mix with oil and vinegar.

Index

About the Author

Liza Fosburgh, a Southerner by birth, lives in the wooded Taconic Hills of New York. She is the author of *Soups & Stews for Fall and Winter Days* and numerous books of fiction, including award-winning novels for young adults, as well as nonfiction articles for magazines and newspapers. Her interests include cooking, gardening, and caring for several dogs and cats.